A
Christ-Centered
HOME

A STORY OF HOPE & HEALING
FOR EVERY FAMILY IN EVERY SITUATION

HANNAH, LEAH & ISAIAH
with Ephraim, Mary & Ezra
STODDARD

JOSEPH SMITH®
FOUNDATION

🔒 Joseph Smith Foundation®

Joseph Smith Foundation is an organization focused on supporting and contributing to projects founded in the words of Jesus Christ. Those contributing to *Joseph Smith Foundation* projects are members of The Church of Jesus Christ of Latter-day Saints, but the foundation is not sponsored by the Church. *Joseph Smith Foundation* projects include documentary films, Latter-day Answers, ZionTube, InspiraWiki, FAQs, Papers, Audio, Ebooks and much more.

www.JosephSmithFoundation.org

Published by:
Joseph Smith Foundation®
Salem, UT, USA

1st printing

Interior Design: Leah M. Stoddard, Isaiah M. Stoddard
Cover Design: Leah M. Stoddard, L. Hannah Stoddard

Thanks & Contribution: Jim F. & Margaret J. Stoddard, Cameron & Kimberly W. Smith, Julie A. & Natalie Smith

Library of Congress Control Number: 2022905527

ISBN: 978-163752348-3

Printed in the USA

A
Christ-Centered
HOME

A STORY OF HOPE & HEALING
FOR EVERY FAMILY IN EVERY SITUATION

HANNAH, LEAH & ISAIAH
with Ephraim, Mary & Ezra Stoddard

Dedication
To Dad

ASSISTANT EDITORS:

Margaret J. Stoddard

Jean M. Courtright

Jennifer L. Hernández

Malissa H. Cochran

Sarah M. Nyberg

Threesa L. Cummings

RaeLyn Stoddard

REVIEWERS & CONTRIBUTORS:

Julie A. Smith

Kimberly W. Smith

Nicole D. Reeder

Mary M. Stoddard

Alexis P. Dollar

Sorena Marble

Sera M. Smith

JOSEPH SMITH® FOUNDATION

Do *you want help building your own* CHRIST-CENTERED *home?*

CONTENTS

CHAPTER
One

DAD'S FINAL PLEADING

*"The most important of the Lord's work you will ever do
will be within the walls of your own homes."*[1]

— *Harold B. Lee*

"You can't go home. You are going to die anytime." The emergency room doctor was sympathetic, but firm and resolute. "It isn't safe." He paused. "I'm sorry, but you may only have a few hours."

"Do we stay? Or do we go?" Our Dad, his mother, and Hannah sat grappling with these questions in the emergency room at the Utah Valley Hospital in Provo, Utah. Dad was battling an aggressive form of non-smokers stage 4 lung cancer that was slowly closing off his lungs and shutting down other organs. The simple act of breathing was agonizingly painful and almost impossible. Following over five months of intense suffering, he had come to the emergency room—yet again—after his liver began malfunctioning, and he had increasing difficulty breathing. Tests revealed a possible blood clot in his liver and extraordinary levels of pleural and pericardial effusion—fluid accumulating around his heart and lungs at an alarming rate, compressing both. There was no known medical cure for the

---

1 Harold B. Lee, *Strengthening the Home* pamphlet, 1973.

effusion, and the cancer was too advanced for any natural or conventional treatment.

It was sometime between midnight and 3 a.m. on May 12, 2021, and everyone was exhausted from sleep deprivation, long caretaking hours, and the overall desperation and uncertainty of the situation. Dad was doubled over in excruciating pain.

A dying man wants to be surrounded by his family—but policies instituted due to COVID-19 allowed only two visitors to stay with Dad in the hospital. Looking at Hannah and his mother, Dad's eyes asked, *"What should we do?"* Finally, after a few heaving breaths, he turned back to the doctor. "I'm not . . . staying here. If I only have . . . a few hours . . . I'm going home . . . have to see my kids. . . . I'll come back . . . but I *have* to see them again."

The doctor paused and assessed the man on the bed before him, sighing. *"Didn't he realize the danger he was in?"* If he let James Stoddard go home, he likely would *not* be coming back. After a few more exchanges, he shrugged his shoulders and gave up. There were still more rounds to complete, and he didn't have time to argue. After signing forms releasing hospital staff from any liability, nurses finally removed Dad's IV and helped him into a wheelchair, shaking their heads in pity for the man who was so determined to see his kids again.

Only about half of the family were able to be home when Dad returned from the hospital. The children who were present—Hannah, Leah, Isaiah, and Ephraim—soberly headed upstairs to the master bedroom and gathered around him, barely able to grasp the gravity of the situation. Dad had been really sick, and doctors had given hopeless verdicts from the very beginning. Frankly, he should have been dead months before—but was it *really* his time to go? Isaiah, our resident 'tech guy,' set up a video camera to capture what might be Dad's final words. We waited in anticipation: *"What was he about to say?"*

What would you say to your beloved children if you only had one final goodbye? You will not be there when some of them graduate or get married—so many life milestones. You will not be able to meet their children—your future grandchildren. What would you want them to remember once you were gone?

Snapshot from the video with Dad's last words

In between sips of electrolyte to counter his dangerously unstable levels, our Dad counseled his children—ranging from six to 26 years old—with these words:

> What I would ask is that everyone keeps the legacy going. Don't forget to stand in the forefront in the cause of truth. Everybody has weaknesses, and everyone makes mistakes—but you've got to overlook that as much as you can and just try to work together.
>
> Happiness doesn't come from partying, or having fun, or breaking the rules. Joy and happiness come from serving God with all your heart. I'm pleading with everybody to keep the work going. Keep the Joseph Smith Foundation going, help defend the Restoration. . . . The Lord knows. I've told Him I'm willing to suffer anything I'm capable of handling to be here with you guys, to keep the work going.

Dad's comments were slow, interrupted by pauses to regain his breath. Again and again, he kept reiterating:

> I just want to tell everybody that I love you guys. Always remind the little kids that I love them. That I would do anything honorable to help them. . . . Try to remember

all of the things I have taught. At the end of the day, don't forget: I love you guys.

When it came time for Dad to return to the hospital, each of us gave him a tight hug. We tried to smile bravely through tears as we looked into each other's eyes. We seemed to communicate without words, all feeling the same question: *"Could we keep the legacy alive on our own?"*

Dad's Legacy

How do you measure the impact of a life—the influence left behind in history? More often than not, this question can be answered through the rising generation—the children. What foundation was left to build upon? What legacy did one's children inherit to carry into the future?

Our Dad, James F. Stoddard III, is known as the founder of the Joseph Smith Foundation, the author of four books, and the producer of eight documentary films. During his life, he gave numerous lectures and firesides, as well as teaching as an instructor at the Provo Missionary Training Center (MTC). Dad published papers on a variety of subjects and served in countless church callings throughout the years. He coached basketball and instructed in private, public, religious, corporate, and home education. In his 'spare' time, he built Highland Cathedral Estate—a planned family retreat and learning facility with perennial gardens and walking trails, specializing in experimental farming techniques and four-season food production. Over time, we have accumulated a folder with letters, emails, and notes from local leaders to reactivated church members, all thankful for his service and testimony. When he spoke at various events and conferences, he was constantly swarmed with men and women who sought him out. Weighed down with burning questions, they were willing to stand in line for hours to hear Dad's insights, experience, hope, and comforting perspective. He couldn't even take a restroom break without someone stopping him to talk.

But we knew him as *Dad*—the Dad who never invested time in a hobby without involving his kids. The Dad who started numerous businesses as family projects, the Dad who took his kids with him everywhere he went, and the Dad who challenged, corrected, and cherished us. From a very young age, Dad felt that he had a mission to perform. But in this search for purpose, he hit upon a secret that many forget: his mission to change the world would be performed with and through his *family*.

As a Christian people, we care deeply about devoting our lives to God. We talk about 'building Zion' and a millennial day of peace, following the Prophet Joseph Smith's admonition: "We ought to have the building up of Zion as our greatest object."[2] But as a people, we have in large part forgotten the simple fact that the home—dedicated families led by righteous fathers and mothers— is our vehicle and secret weapon in the war between light and darkness—a war that began in the premortal life. Our struggles and failures in building Zion, defending liberty, and spreading truth in the world today are in large part due to the fact that our homes are not in order. Individuals are fighting detached and alone, instead of uniting with designed teams that God purposely sent to earth *together*. Our homes are broken and divided.

Dad seemed to be born with an innate understanding that he had a mission—a calling that was not given to him alone. It was a *family* calling. Many are familiar with Dad's work—but *how* these accomplishments came to be is an untold story of sacrifice, trial, faith, and miracles.

Life was never meant to be easy. Our family has been through many of the ups and downs that challenge all faithful Latter-day Saint families: divorce, death, teen rebellion, pornography addiction, and more. But our Dad did something uniquely different from any other home we have observed—he invested hours, days, weeks, and years into studying forgotten teachings from inspired prophets and presidents of the Church of Jesus Christ of Latter-day Saints. Then, he decided to try something revolutionary! Together, he and his family would apply these teachings and live the counsel practically. Not just infusing gospel principles into school and

---

2   Joseph Smith, Discourse, circa 26 June and circa 4 August 1839–A, as reported by Willard Richards, p. 70, The Joseph Smith Papers.

career, but actually building our entire lives—diet, education, work, recreation, entertainment, etc.—around, on, and with the Rock of Revelation. He 'experimented on the word' by creating a home with exceptionally high standards, a home focused on consecrated service, a home that became a productive center for missionary work, entrepreneurial business, and worldwide teaching. From our family team—a Dad with his kids—came the Joseph Smith Foundation and many other projects that point members to gospel principles, blessing the lives of thousands in the Church today.

The Lord needs more homes that are mobilized and equipped to defend the Gospel of Jesus Christ in our day and age. Your own home is a secret weapon that may be a sleeping giant with unimaginable potential. *You* can make a difference—in spite of horrific trials—when your family embraces true principles drawn from the scriptures. Our home was led by a righteous father, but these principles can be adapted for any home. A mother can build such a home—or an uncle, an aunt, a grandparent, or a sibling.

This book is our family's testimony of God's work in our lives. We aren't perfect, and we aren't immune to life's challenges. If you are expecting a story of 'rainbows and unicorns'—a picture-perfect, flawless family—you should probably close this book and find something else to read. If you choose to keep reading, be forewarned that this is a realistic story of celebratory victories, but also dark nights of despair—sunny days with beaming smiles, and then stormy, depressing days with heart-rending tears. This is a story that embraces the challenges that face many families today: divorce, mental illness, abuse, loss of a child, miscarriage, children with special needs, cancer, slander and betrayal, and financial hardship. Some days, we felt our story was merely the saga of a tenacious struggle to keep going even when we were breaking.

But the God of Abraham, Isaac, and Jacob is *our* God, and this is our testimony that He *will* prevail. We have discovered for ourselves that the Gospel of Jesus Christ holds answers that solve even the most difficult, the most heart-breaking, and the most traumatic of situations. We want to share this hope—this 'good news'—with you!

CHAPTER
Two

THE LONE PILGRIM

"These all died in faith, not having received the promises, but having seen them afar off, and were persuaded of them, and embraced them, and confessed that they were strangers and pilgrims on the earth. . . . But now they desire a better country, that is, an heavenly: wherefore God is not ashamed to be called their God . . ."

— *Hebrews 11:13-16*

D ad always felt he was searching for more. Usernames or passwords sometimes reveal one's passion—or lack of it. Dad time and time again chose "lone pilgrim." Growing up, he was burning with questions—searching to discover where he fit—his purpose, his real identity. That journey, in many ways, began when he was 13 years old.

Years later, he could still remember staring up at the ceiling in his room—weighing what seemed to his youthful mind a perfectly logical direction: "*Should I collect baseball cards? Or am I supposed to do something else?*" he wondered. "*What should I do with my life?*" He would later recall:

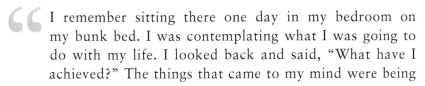 I remember sitting there one day in my bedroom on my bunk bed. I was contemplating what I was going to do with my life. I looked back and said, "What have I achieved?" The things that came to my mind were being

in the band, being the Student of the Year in 7th grade, having good grades, etc. Then I thought, "Yea[h], but what's important?"

The boy's soul-searching question was sincere, and the Lord answered. In an unmistakable moment of revelation, he felt the instruction come: *"Study the Gospel so well that no matter who speaks, you will not be deceived."*

The guidance was so clear and certain that he got up, walked out of his bedroom, and found his mother: "Mom, I'm supposed to study the Gospel. Where should I start?" Forever after, he would express unmeasurable gratitude for the inspired direction she took at this definitive moment. Turning to their bookshelf, she pulled out *Teachings of the Prophet Joseph Smith*, *Doctrines of Salvation*, *Mormon Doctrine*, *Answers to Gospel Questions*, and a few other volumes. "Start here," she said.

Returning to his room, the young lad set his baseball cards to the side and began poring over the books. He started with a determination to read 30 minutes a day. "*If I read my scriptures for 30 minutes every day, I bet I would know a lot in a few years,*" he thought. However, the more he learned, the more he realized all he did not know, and his goal promptly increased to between one to three hours per day.

Hour by hour, a new world opened up to him—a new way of approaching life, a new understanding of eternity. He read all three volumes of *Doctrines of Salvation*, the Book of Mormon half a dozen times, all five volumes of *Answers to Gospel Questions*, *Teachings of Ezra Taft Benson*, the Old Testament, the New Testament several times, the Doctrine and Covenants two or three times, the Pearl of Great Price several times—and as he later wrote, "all the other books I could get my hands on. My freshman and sophomore years I was [studying like] a madman! My confidence grew and grew, and I learned that the Lord knew who I was, and I felt like I had big things to do."

~

Each of us has a specific purpose for our life. If we ask with a sincere heart, the Lord will guide us with the instruction, opportunities, & connections we need to fulfill our mission.

~

Shortly thereafter, Dad's commitment led him, at age 14, to another experience when he came to comprehend the holiness, nobility, honor, integrity, dignity, and—above all—*love*, that embodies the character of God. He gained a certain witness that Jesus Christ lives. Later, he would share with us that one of the most profound insights he gained from that experience is the power of pure love. He was being bullied in school by a few former friends, and the daily torture had planted bitterness in his heart. However, during this experience, his anger was entirely washed away. He loved even those bullies! Dad would spend the rest of his life endeavoring to recapture and enjoy that peace again and again, urging his children to likewise follow this path to the Tree of Life—to taste the priceless fruit.

However, life was certainly not all study. Jimmy, as he was known, put in hours playing basketball, helping his dad, and doing all manner of work to assist his large family in making ends meet. He and his younger brothers spent long days, in all types of weather, moving irrigation lines, unloading frozen fish, and shoveling coal. He also loved sports and soon discovered a natural talent there. However, he never allowed his recreation to compromise his standards. One friend remembered:

> In little league baseball, we were on the same team. He was the pitcher, and I was the catcher. He threw the fastest and nobody could hit his strikes. So I often went home with a sore left hand. Ouch! He was the best.

> He refused to play on the all-star team because the games were on Sunday and he chose to keep the Sabbath day holy. I remember once we had Family Home Evening with his family and we watched *Chariots of Fire*. Eric Liddell was the fastest man in the world. However, he wouldn't run in the Paris Olympics because he wouldn't run on Sunday and felt it to be a holy day, the Lord's day. Due to his faith, he was able to run a different race on a different day and won gold. He would not sacrifice his integrity or faith in God for any cost.

> At the end of the movie, Jimmy stood up and pointed to the TV. Looking at his brothers he said boldly, "This is why we don't play ball on Sunday!" He refused the baseball all-star team more than once with no regrets or doubt. I always respected him for his testimony.

"Be Good . . . But Don't Tell Anyone"

Before this time, Dad had struggled with being 'different' in 4th and 5th grades. Classmates began dividing into 'popular' versus 'unpopular' groups. While his former friends became 'cool,' Dad fell into the shunned category, and he was teased in school for his standards. Dad's family also struggled at times financially, and the 'cool kids' used monetary disparity as another strike against young Jimmy. When the basketball teams were being chosen in 6th grade, Dad stayed after school hoping with all his heart he could make the team. He missed the bus, but he didn't care. This was more important than the two to three mile walk home in the cold January snow. Dad's heart sank, however, when he realized the coaches had chosen two of his former friends (turned bullies) to choose the players. Dad didn't make the team. Depressed and near tears, he walked home in the frigid weather, feeling as though he might freeze. The government school environment of demeaning competition, prejudice, bullying, and loneliness was something he never forgot. Ever after, Dad strictly *never* tolerated his children nagging, excluding, or belittling a sibling in our home.

Ostracization continued the next school year in 7th grade, but then something changed—a deceptive event that he would forever use as an object lesson and warning for his children. One day he was standing—broken and hurting—in the school bathroom when an idea occurred to his mind. It was a brilliant plan of his own—or so he thought. *"Everyone teases you because you are different. You can be good, but why does anyone else need to know? Be committed, be consecrated—but just don't tell anyone. Then you will be popular!"*

How many of us have fallen into the same trap—hiding our true feelings, desires, and personality because we know we may be mocked or ostracized? Our Dad would often tell us this story with a shake of his head at his gullibility. "I was just a kid. I thought it was brilliant. I didn't realize what was really going on." So for the next several years, Jimmy hid his light under a bushel. He was still a good kid. He was top of his seminary class, an Eagle Scout, and valedictorian. When classmates tried to shove pornography in his face, he consistently refused to look. To this day, he is one of the few men we know who can honestly say that they have never succumbed to the temptation of looking at pornography. Jimmy was friends with everyone—

the nerds and the cool kids. But did anyone know he went home and studied his scriptures for hours every day? Did anyone know he devoured Church books like other kids consumed comics and cartoons? Did anyone know his one and only experience with a video game was when he purchased a new release and then gave it away after one try, because he felt he had more important work in which he should invest his time? Did anyone know he would read Jane Austen or other classic literature— dreaming of restoring art, music, dance, and theater defined by honor and nobility? Did anyone know that the popular music of the day made him feel uncomfortable? Did anyone know he was pondering deep doctrines and life's purpose on the school bus? Did anyone know this high schooler was yearning to build Zion—to make a difference in the world? Not really.

But strangely, the persecution he had been enduring in 7th grade ceased, and he became quite popular. He didn't do anything 'bad,' but he didn't stir the pot for good either—and

Visiting the Berlin Wall during his high school years, after traveling to play basketball in Germany

everyone *liked* him! He was an exceptionally talented basketball player—with many impressive accomplishments. He was good-looking, funny, creative, friendly, and kind. He could ask any girl on a date in the school, and she would accept. He was living 'the life!'

Did I Waste My Life?

After a severely sprained ankle during his senior year of high school, a relationship break-up, and a series of other humbling events, dots began to connect in Dad's mind. He later recognized that God was stripping him of his pride during this time to prepare him to refocus on the true purpose of life. Another major milestone occurred when he entered the Missionary Training Center (MTC) on Wednesday, October 18, 1989, less than two weeks shy of his 19th birthday.

Dad was called to serve in the California Ventura Mission, Korean speaking. One day, shortly before entering the MTC, he found himself in the car with one of his cousins who playfully reached over the seat and grabbed his scriptures. As she began thumbing through the pages, her demeanor turned

into one of surprise and curiosity. Looking up in amazement, she exclaimed, "Jimmy, your scriptures are *completely* marked up!" Dad didn't mention the list of other Church books he had read or the several times he had already read the entire standard works. Looking at him curiously, his cousin added, "All this time you've been seriously invested in studying the gospel?? I never knew this side of you!"

Her words cut Dad to the heart. His cousin hadn't known who he really was. She hadn't known his deepest passions and dreams—and neither did most of those in his life so far. Would they have understood anyway? Would he have been slighted and teased? But on the other hand, what lives had remained unchanged for the better because he had hidden what he knew? What had been lost by concealing his studious example or bold witness—regardless of the damage vulnerability would have had on his image? Why didn't he share his light with others, whatever the cost?

Another bombshell soon hit Dad like a ton of bricks. Waking up on his first full day in the MTC, he heard a clear message that he felt was from God: "You have wasted your life." What?! "*But God,*" he murmured. "*I spent hours every day reading the scriptures. I never missed a day! Even when it was really late at night and I had just gotten back in town from a basketball trip and had to go to school the next morning, I still read my scriptures for at least an hour. I was top of my seminary class. I was valedictorian. I worked extremely long hours in the heat and cold for my grandpa, uncles, and parents. What do you mean, I 'wasted' my life?*"

In response, the simple questions came: "But what lasting good have you accomplished? How many have you converted and brought to Me? It's not what you achieve for your own life—it's those you help experience a change of heart that really makes the difference."

James F. Stoddard would never be the same again. From that moment, he committed his time, his talents, his energy, his possessions, and everything he had to serve, teach, and lift others. As Dad put on his missionary name tag, he promised the Lord he would never remove a similar engraving on his heart. He was committing to serve a mission for life.

What Do I Do With My Life?

Dad poured everything he had into his two-year mission for the Church of Jesus Christ of Latter-day Saints. A missionary who knew him in the MTC still remembers years later:

Dad (far right) on his mission

" I recall him being obedient. After a few weeks the other companionships in our district started sleeping in a little bit, but not Elder Stoddard and myself. We honored all the rules, etc. I saw him as very focused on the gospel and a very quick learner even in Korean language. . . . He always enjoyed the sports during that hour, and focused a lot on playing basketball and volleyball. He was very proud of his high school basketball background at Salmon and Littlefield. . . . He was clearly prepared to be a missionary, and delved into all he could learn as fast as he could learn.

. . . The main thing I really remember is the level of detail and the depth in what he knew and wanted to learn. It's like the rest of us were working on a BA level gospel knowledge and he was seeking a PhD.[1]

---

1 Dad's former companion also commented, "I remember one time we were doing a round-robin "What we are thankful for" in our class time with our teachers, and we were in the MTC over Thanksgiving. All of

Dad served for two years, and would forever remember the lessons he learned as an elder and district leader, serving a wide range of families with diverse backgrounds. Hours were spent each day—and night—helping struggling missionaries.

Returning home in 1991, the main question on his mind became: "*Where do I go from here?*" An entry from his journal on October 23, 1991, reads:

 It looks as if I have been home a week. It has been a big adjustment, but it's been fun. We're trying to decide where I should go to school and work and what kind of car to get and most of all w[h]ere to get the money for it all. There are so many things I need to get done. . . . I guess the biggest difference between here and the mission field is that in the field you are serving. Serving the Lord, the people, the missionaries (you're almost forced into it). Here, the opportunities are there, but it's [not] quite the same.

The next day, Dad decided to attend Utah Valley Community College (now Utah Valley University), and play college basketball. Dad *loved* basketball—it was an inseparable part of his identity and passion! He would always maintain that basketball and other similar sports were exceptional opportunities to learn character, teamwork, and discipline. But Dad and his brothers didn't just enjoy basketball—they were talented at the sport, and Dad's patriarchal blessing talked about increasing his talents. "I've decided to do it," he recorded in his journal. "Now I'm going to go all the way and give it my best shot."

However, only three days later, an unexpected event changed the course of his life forever. On October 27, 1991, two days before his 21st birthday, his mom handed him a VHS tape cassette

---

us were saying things we [were] grateful for. About the second or third time around the room, your dad talked about how he was thankful for his parents and their examples, and it touched him enough that as he was saying it, his lips were quivering. It struck us all, we all suddenly felt the spirit and emotions, and suddenly our session was all of us in tears about the many things we were grateful for, and family being one of them."

Dad (far left) with brothers JP and Jared

titled *America's Godly Heritage*. The presentation was produced only a year before by David Barton, a young teacher and the founder of WallBuilders[2]—an organization dedicated to historical research on America's Christian foundations. In the video, Barton presented historical evidence that the Founding Fathers were God-fearing Christians, rather than self-serving atheists, and that America's founding documents were rooted in a spiritual, biblical foundation. Barton revealed the progressive effort to remove God from our education, culture, business, and public policy by rewriting our historical narratives to eliminate Christianity.

Within the space of only a few hours, *everything* changed for Dad. He was overwhelmed with a new vision for his life—a cause God wanted him to undertake as his own. Dad was on fire as his mind began to comprehend the battlefield before him! The adversary was not only removing Jesus Christ from American

2   "WallBuilders is an organization dedicated to presenting America's forgotten history and heroes, with an emphasis on the moral, religious, and constitutional foundation on which America was built." (Description from WallBuilders.com)

history, but eliminating God from *every aspect* of life and thought: science, psychology, education, journalism, the news, movies, music, and so forth. Dad received the impression he should become a teacher—an opportunity to help put God back into education. Writing in his journal that night, Dad recorded:

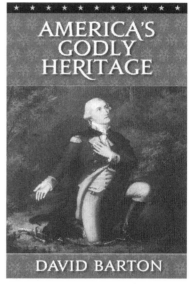

> 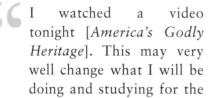 I watched a video tonight [*America's Godly Heritage*]. This may very well change what I will be doing and studying for the next little bit. This has really got me fired up. Something's got to be done about this. We need to get the seminary teachers, stake presidents, (leaders) involved in this. Why not put an article in the Ensign[?] We need to speak up and take a stand. It will take me a while to study it all out though. I hope I can keep fired up.

A truly successful home and family with a mission requires a father and/or mother who has a specific vision or calling revealed from the Lord for the family. Sacrifice is required to obtain that knowledge from God.

With the weight of this new calling, Dad realized that sacrifices had to be made. He was working at a video store, but quit because of the "pornographic video covers." Dad refused to place himself in situations that could potentially cause him to compromise his morals. "We need the money bad, but you have to keep your standards," he wrote in his journal. At the same time, Dad made another hard decision: he abandoned his plans to play basketball in college. "I've decided to not play basketball after all. It was a tough decision, but I just have too many things that I need to be doing, and I need to get doing them."

Dad gave the Lord His heart. It was *not* easy, but he trusted that, in the end, it would all be worth it. The Lord in turn answered, leading him in the right direction.

Dad shifted his focus, and applied to attend Brigham Young University. After a period of prayer and reflection, he began pursuing a degree in social sciences. His classes drove him to immerse himself in a thorough study of the scriptures, as he waded through a myriad of progressive philosophies challenging him at every turn. He also began a thorough study of the Book of Mormon, highlighting the themes of freedom and liberty.

Then as Dad began attending classes on campus in Provo, Utah, he found himself shocked by some of the ideologies he encountered. Writing in his journal in 1992:

 Since I have been at BYU, I have been taught especially evolution and Communism, socialism, welfare state, etc. But also humanism, rationalism, and other isms. Well, I haven't known at all what could be done about it because all of the professors and students believe it and take it all in like the gospel.

Searching to find forgotten answers, Dad would visit old thrift stores in his free time, and buy every book written by a President of the Church he could get his hands on. He acquired copies of President Ezra Taft Benson's talks on tape, listening to them over and over again while driving to campus. He just wanted to know the truth! After attending classes during the day, he would return home and study the words of inspired prophets late into the night, searching for clarity and inspiration on every topic. Often, two ideologies would be debated in class. Confused, he would return home, pull out his scriptures and books, and search to discover which position was correct. Almost always, he found that the answer was *neither*—the Lord's teachings had not even been discussed or broached in class! Asking questions, engaging in debate, receiving personal revelation, and devoting time to intense study and prayer, laid the foundation for Dad's unique understanding of key battlelines and attacks in opposition to the Gospel of Jesus Christ in the 20th and 21st centuries. Dad would use this training for the rest of his life—especially after beginning the Joseph Smith Foundation.

Men and women of God do not stand idly by—
they take initiative and act.

Not one to remain silent, Dad tried his best to initiate reform. He spent hours in long discussions with students—endeavoring to share the teachings of the Presidents of the Church. He wrote letters to the college leadership at all levels, working to bring awareness of many classes and professors who were teaching against the traditional positions and teachings of the Church. He attended conservative clubs. He talked to professor after professor, and dean after dean, hoping to find someone willing to help. He may have been only a 22-year-old returned missionary, but he was confident that the Lord would reveal the next step if he did everything immediately possible within his power and sphere of influence. The Lord always reveals line upon line, precept upon precept, based on obedience to each instruction.

Lucifer's primary strategy to obtain power and
influence is removing God from our society, culture, &
government. We must fight to put God back into every
aspect of our society.

Dad with James & Leah building a Lego castle

As Dad studied, turning repeatedly to the scriptures, he discovered the answers to many of society's complex questions. The simple and prophetic answers to mankind's dilemmas had been neglected and ignored, gathering dust on forgotten bookshelves. How could he share this newfound treasure of knowledge and wisdom with the world? That was the million-dollar question!

Starting a Family

In 1994, Dad married and immediately began juggling work, school, and then a family. Hannah was born in 1995, followed by James (b. 1996), Leah (b. 1998), Asael (b. 1999), Joseph (b. 2001), Isaiah (b. 2003), Ephraim (b. 2005), Mary (b. 2008),

Dad with Joseph, putting in the flagpole for his birthday

Ezra (b. 2011), and Eliza (b. 2014). Dad taught high school classes and coached basketball near the Kaibab Paiute Indian Reservation for a time before returning to college to pursue a career in computer science. His brother encouraged him to move to California to begin working as a software engineer for Agilent Technologies, a job obtained through a series of miracles. Later, our family moved to Colorado before finally migrating back to Utah in 2006.

Life was busy: diapers, bills, health issues, church callings, careers, etc. But after Hannah attended one year of kindergarten, coming home 'engaged' to a boyfriend and having acquired rebellious attitudes and progressive worldviews, Dad and Mom decided to homeschool. There was never a dull moment around the house!

Dad with Hannah, James, Leah, and Asael after he brought boxes from his work and built a fort in our bedroom for us to sleep in

Two main principles served as the bedrock of our home:

1. We follow God's laws, and
2. We defend the truth and teach the Gospel.

In our school room, Mom hung a large whiteboard which read: "The Purpose of Our Life & School is to (1) Become Like God, (2) Help Others Become Like God." While we filled out math worksheets or completed spelling tests, we were continually reminded *why* we were studying.

A successful home will be led by parents who are grounded in the word of God & who build their home on the rock of scripture & divine revelation.

Dad reading 'Illustrated Stories from Church History' with Mary, Ezra, & Eliza

Dad began applying the standards and teachings he had learned from his study throughout his early years and experiences as a college student. The Lord also blessed us in meeting new friends—many from different faiths—and encountering books, magazines, and talks advocating a return to scriptural principles and higher standards in culture.

Dad scoured video stores looking for good, wholesome movies. Studying the Gospel was heavily emphasized and incorporated into our curriculum. Homeschooling, adopting scriptural principles for relationships, raising music standards based on the teachings of Presidents David O. McKay, Harold B. Lee, and Ezra Taft Benson, learning folk and country dances, studying scientific evidence that vindicated the revelations, and so forth—all contributed to making our family unique. Unlike too many fathers, who feel their role is limited to bringing home a paycheck and participating in a few family activities, Dad's first priority was his family. He poured all of his extra time, energy, thought, prayers, and study, into teaching and rearing a family to the best of his ability.

Dad and Eliza making faces

HELPING US FIND ANSWERS IN THE SCRIPTURES

Mary remembers: I remember one time a few years ago, I was sitting outside when Dad came out of our house and started talking to me. At first, we were just chatting about how the day had been, and then we started talking about gospel stuff. He asked me why we were here. I answered, "So we can get tested and grow." "That may be true, too," he said, "But, it isn't the main reason. Here, open up your scriptures." We went through different verses until it suddenly clicked. "Oh, we are here to have joy." That was the way Dad taught us. He didn't just say, "This is the reason," but guided us through it and let us figure it out for ourselves.

In the back of Dad's mind, he never forgot the bigger picture—the need to reach an increasingly degenerate world with a message of hope—the need to build Zion! After giving a fireside on the Book of Mormon in the early 2000s, he created the 'For

One of Dad's favorite pictures with Hannah as a baby

Our Day' model and began writing a book on 'Book of Mormon Parallels.'[3] Putting his software skills to use, he created a simple family website with history from our ancestors, Christ-centered holiday ideas, providential miracles from the past, and a wholesome family movie list. In addition to sharing whatever knowledge he gained with us, Dad did his best to share this knowledge through every possible avenue with those outside our home.

A foundation in scripture was being laid for our family to discover our place—our role in sustaining the Restoration. But to truly uncover that path, a devastating tragedy would turn our world upside down, causing us to refocus and dig deeper in discovering our family's purpose.

---

3 Dad's research would later become the *For Our Day* DVD series and timelines, currently available through the Joseph Smith Foundation.

CHAPTER
Three

LOSING OUR LITTLE WARRIOR

*"O my son, he hath blessed me in raising thee up to be a
servant unto me, in saving my house from death."*

— JST Genesis 48:8

It was February 27, 2005—a bright Sunday morning—but
we were sick with the flu and cooped up in bed. We were
huddled upstairs in our room watching the animated *Pilgrim's
Progress* when a firetruck and ambulance pulled up in front of
our home. At first we were curious, and then *very* confused as we
heard a great commotion and anxious voices downstairs! What
was happening? Seven-year-old Leah, who had been throwing
up in the bathroom just a few minutes before, crawled over to
the top of the stairs and saw a group of adults hovering over a
little shape at the bottom. They were murmuring in low voices,
handing each other objects and an oxygen tank. Everything was
tense and urgent. A few minutes later, Dad came upstairs and
opened the door to our bedroom. We were shocked to see that
his face was wet and covered with tears. We had never seen Dad
cry before. He simply said, "Pray, guys. Pray for Joseph." And
then he was gone.

Hours later, Hannah woke up to the sound of Mom weeping
in another room, and it sounded as though she was talking with
someone on the phone: "Are you sure? Are you *sure*?!"

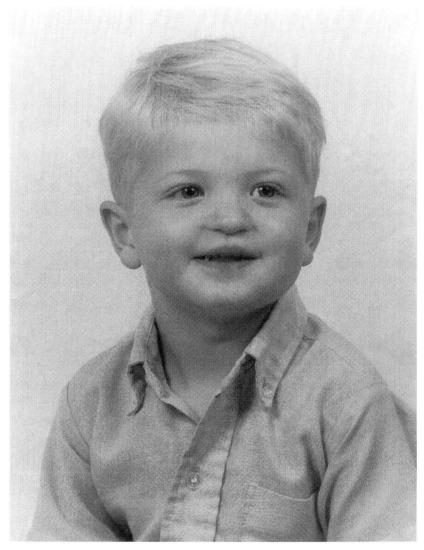

Sometimes it is easy to forget that all great miracles and accomplishments throughout history have been forged in the fire of sacrifice and suffering. God uses adversity in our lives to shape us, to drive us to our knees—ultimately revealing a forgotten identity and hidden destiny through humility. No true greatness has been gained through ease and comfort, and this principle has certainly been true for our family!

The Lord Visits His People in Affliction

Four years previous to this Sunday emergency, we were living in California—having moved near San Francisco after our Dad felt impressed that our family needed to live in that specific location. When Mom went into labor at the beginning of July 2001, we didn't think much of it. We were just ecstatic that we got to sleep overnight in a homemade tent made from blankets and chairs at our Uncle Jared and Aunt Kaylene's house! We also got to play with a set of plastic dump trucks and flatbed trailers—common Stoddard toys among all the cousins! The first indication that something was amiss came with a phone call from the hospital. It was Dad—his voice was calm, but with a tone of underlying soberness. "Mom had the baby! It's a boy, but he's having trouble breathing. Say some prayers!" We gathered together as siblings with our uncle, aunt, and cousins, and prayed. And then we waited.

Joseph Fielding Stoddard was born July 2, 2001, at 5:16 a.m.—the anniversary of the day Joseph Smith finished the Joseph Smith Translation of the Bible (168 years previous), as well as the anniversary of the day our American forefathers formally declared independence from Britain in 1776. He was named for Joseph of Egypt and the Prophet Joseph Smith, as well as Dad's doctrinal hero, Joseph Fielding Smith.

Unfortunately, our little Joseph was born with a ventricular septal defect—his heart had a small hole in it. Joseph was rushed to the ICU, and a few days later our parents learned that an open heart surgery would be necessary. Ideally, the doctors strongly recommended waiting 3-6 months, but when Joseph stopped eating two weeks later, he was rushed to the emergency room. The hospital staff knew they couldn't wait any longer, and the dangerous procedure was scheduled.

The emotional trauma of this experience never left Dad and Mom; even 20 years later, Dad could never think back to those days in the hospital without crying. After the first open heart surgery, Joseph's heart rate hovered from the high 180s to 218 for almost two days. Hospital staff attempted to remedy the

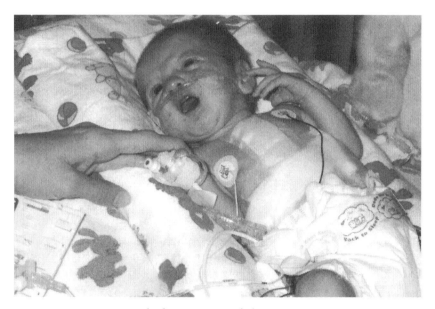

Joseph during one of the surgeries

situation by completely undressing him and placing a cold towel on his head with a fan over him. The room was frigid, and our parents were still chilled even wearing their heavy coats. As they watched little Joseph stretched out, naked and freezing, their hearts broke—he was white as a ghost. Joseph's high heart rate was registering on every doctor's monitor throughout the ICU. Miraculously, his heart rate finally did come down.

Can words describe the emotions of a father and mother watching their precious infant endure excruciating pain— screaming as nurses struggle to insert an IV or perform another procedure? Many times Joseph's eyes would suddenly freeze wide open, pain etched across his face, while every hair stood straight on end. However, you could see the warrior within him fighting back and refusing to give in. His jaw would set firm, but he often refused to cry. In fact, Dad and Mom were often worried that they wouldn't know when he was in pain, because he was so tough. The trauma was definite, however. For the rest of Joseph's life, if he ever saw an adult wearing a white coat approach him, he would immediately begin shaking and try to hide. But, as the Lord taught the people of Alma:

> . . . the Lord seeth fit to chasten his people; yea he trieth their patience and their faith. . . . I will also ease the burdens which are put upon your shoulders . . . that ye may stand as witnesses for me hereafter, and that ye may know of a surety that I, the Lord God, do visit my people in their afflictions.[1]

God *did* "visit" our family. He was there, even in that lonely California hospital. A year or so earlier, when Dad was praying about whether he should accept a job offer in California, the words came: "I need you in San Francisco." Those words came back vividly to his mind now in 2001 as he waited in the hospital hallway for Joseph's blood to be typed for the operation. Doctors told him that patients were traveling to *this* very hospital from all over the world to have Dr. V. Mohan Reddy and Dr. Frank Hanley, world-famous surgeons, operate. Learning about another family whose child had been operated on three times before the parents finally decided to come to that hospital to be treated by "the best," our family knew *why* the Lord directed Dad to move here.

Another miracle occurred when trying to find blood for Joseph's operation. Joseph's blood type was A-, while the rest of our family all had type A+. Our Dad was impressed to give Joseph a blessing beforehand that he would receive clean blood as well as be given assistance with the recovery. A short time later, a donor was found. When Joseph's heart rate eventually stabilized following the operation, our family understood and felt the power of priesthood blessings and answered prayers. Dad had been impressed to pray for a safe recovery long before we knew there would be challenges—the Lord had anticipated each step before the need arose.

A year and a half later, a second open heart surgery was deemed necessary for Joseph. Again, Joseph was given another blessing which spoke of the natural course of events being altered by faith. Quoting from Dad's journal:

---

1   Mosiah 23:21, 24:14.

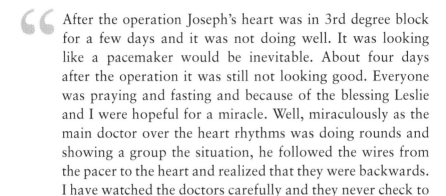 After the operation Joseph's heart was in 3rd degree block for a few days and it was not doing well. It was looking like a pacemaker would be inevitable. About four days after the operation it was still not looking good. Everyone was praying and fasting and because of the blessing Leslie and I were hopeful for a miracle. Well, miraculously as the main doctor over the heart rhythms was doing rounds and showing a group the situation, he followed the wires from the pacer to the heart and realized that they were backwards. I have watched the doctors carefully and they never check to make sure the pacer wires are right. It is not something that I have ever seen. This was one of the miracles.

Dad felt he was getting sick right before the operation and he pleaded for healing because he couldn't bear the thought of not being present with Joseph in the hospital. At that time, Dad was experiencing some serious health issues, and any cold or flu would incapacitate him for an extended period, often requiring antibiotics and other medications. But the following day, his symptoms were almost entirely gone! Joseph also recovered from this second surgery quickly, and our parents were able to bring him home after only seven and a half days. Babies on either side of Joseph caught an infection, but Joseph curiously remained unharmed. RSV (a common respiratory virus) was spreading throughout the hospital, and when Joseph was moved to the floor, both babies in the next rooms were battling respiratory colds, with one in need of breathing treatments. Again, Joseph did not catch any contagious virus or illness. The Lord did "visit [his] people in their afflictions," and "did strengthen them that they could bear up their burdens . . ."[2]

Trials and miracles teach us to rely on the
Lord and patiently submit.

---

2   Mosiah 24:14-15.

Chef Joseph giving a cooking class on how to make the perfect hamburger

"It is Better This Way"

Joseph brought joy, laughter, and a *lot* of sword fighting into our home. Everything revolved around war, and he was constantly dressed in his plastic "Armor of God" breastplate, sword, and shield. At the same time, he was very loving and affectionate. Throughout the day, he would randomly stop playing, run over to Dad, hug his leg for a minute, and then go back to playing. During meals, he would pull his high chair next to Isaiah's so they could hold hands. Mom kept pulling their chairs apart because baby Isaiah would grab food off Joseph's tray, but Joseph always pushed the chairs back together again.

Joseph was very firm in purpose. If he felt something needed to be done a certain way, nothing could change his mind. He had no fear, and one could sense the sober, mature spirit within him. He also had a sense of humor that was not light-minded—remarkable for a little three-year-old. He could keep everyone laughing with his witty personality, but he wasn't silly. It is uncommon to find someone so strong, yet also tender, loving, and cheerful. We called him our "little soldier of the Lord" and "Soldier Man."

The Lord had a greater purpose in mind for Joseph. On February 27, 2005, Joseph was playing with one of his brothers while most of the kids were recovering from the flu, and Dad and Mom were studying peacefully downstairs. When a small skirmish broke out, Dad dispelled the fighting by taking Joseph with him to another room—our so-called "prophets room" because bookshelves containing our treasured library with hundreds of Church books lined the walls. It was in this special room that Joseph's heart stopped. He was sitting on the sofa next to our Dad when he suddenly slumped over and collapsed.

Pandemonium ensued. Mom called 9-1-1, and Dad began CPR, but his efforts were all in vain. An ambulance came, and Joseph was rushed to the hospital. A priesthood blessing was administered there while the physicians worked for some time at Dad's pleading, trying to revive Joseph's body. Finally, the doctors gave up. "We're very sorry, but he's gone," they tried to explain.[3]

Quietly and calmly, another blessing was given to Joseph's lifeless body, and in a great test of faith, Dad forced his heart to surrender to the will of the Lord. After the blessing, Dad kept trying to revive Joseph's body all on his own—a sacred moment between a devoted father and the lifeless body of his precious son. As he later shared with tears in his eyes: "I wasn't leaving that room until I knew without a shadow of a doubt that I had done everything that I possibly could." When Dad was finally given the assurance that he, as the father, had done everything within his power, that Joseph would not be returning to mortality, and that his little boy had reunited with his loved ones on the other side, he quietly left to call Mom.

At home, Mom cried hysterically. All Dad could say was, "It is better this way." Did Dad want it to be that way? Never! This was a horror beyond anything he had ever expected, and there had been no warning—no time to say goodbye, no time to ensure his little "Soldier Man" knew how much he treasured and adored him.

---

3   Some felt that delayed complications or possibly a medical mistake from one of the previous heart surgeries were the cause of Joseph's death.

"It is better this way." Saying those words from the heart took great faith. Somehow, God had a purpose in mind that our family did not yet understand. If we want to serve God and build His kingdom, we must be prepared to be chastened and refined so we are prepared to do His work.

FINDING A FAITHFUL OLDER BROTHER

Hannah remembers: I'll never forget those hours after learning that Joseph had died. There was a calm, peaceful stillness in our home—it felt just like the temple. We were stunned and shocked. I couldn't cry at first because my little 10-year-old brain was struggling to understand what it all meant—but the deep peace, love, and power I will never forget. Looking back, I can see God preparing our family in the days before Joseph's death. He passed away two days after my 10th birthday. I remember this because on the morning of my birthday, I had gone downstairs with my siblings to watch a movie. Something was working on our hearts that morning, and instead of cartoons, we curiously chose to watch a theater play on the life of William Tyndale and the English Reformation. God was quietly beginning to work in our hearts, changing interests, and teaching us to love and appreciate sacred things.

Healing and tears came years later for me. By this time, we had moved to Utah and started the Joseph Smith Foundation. Deep in my soul growing up, I had desperately longed for a big, older brother. I wrote fictional novels, and nearly every plot contained a recurring theme: the female protagonist had a strong, noble brother who was an example to her. One afternoon, when I was 16 years old, I was alone in our basement office looking at some family pictures of Joseph. Emotion I had never expressed unexpectedly released, and I cried and cried and cried, sitting alone by myself in that office. I missed my brother. I missed the chance to hug him goodbye. I missed seeing him grow up. I missed his strength and stalwart character.

Now I realized he was not gone. He was *still* my brother, and more than that, he was now the big brother I had always longed for.

Our family has been blessed by his support many times. He is not missing in action—he is battling *with* us! He is still watching over our family, and he is involved and intensely interested in the work we are doing.

That day when I was 16, a connection between us was forged. I was his sister, and he wanted me to be strong. He wanted me to have integrity, to keep my standards, to speak for truth, and live a pure life so that one day, I could return to the other side and hear him say, "I'm proud of you, Sis. Well done."

*A family mission encompasses both sides of the veil—
transcending death and separation.*

Value Your Family & Each Moment

Joseph's unexpected death was a turning point in our family's life—but surprisingly, it turned for our *good!* Something about the "valley of the shadow" forced us to reevaluate life and reassess our priorities. We were not prepared to do God's work until we were sufficiently humble and submissive. For our family, Joseph's death changed our perspective on life and what really matters. Dad recorded in his journal on March 24, 2005:

> It has been almost one month since Joseph passed away and it seems like it was yesterday. We have been greatly blessed and it has been a time of growth and learning. Through it all there are two fundamental principles that must not

Leah and Joseph

be forgotten. First, I would be willing to pay thousands of dollars to have Joseph back for even a short time. Unfortunately, that is not how I always acted while he was here. We must work to always have a spirit of appreciation, love and patience here in the home with all of the children.

Second, and closely related, we need to always keep our priorities straight. In the Lord's plan the family is the most important organization and should always take precedence. I preach this all the time, but there are many areas that we could work on and improve. When a child is taken, as Joseph was, there are only two regrets. The first is that we could have had a more heavenly environment while he was here, and second that we could have used the time better. . . . The Lord called him home and His decisions are sometimes difficult, but always the best.

Love was the primary theme that seemed to stir Dad's mind following Joseph's death. "The bottom line is love," Dad wrote in his journal on May 29, 2005. This love and appreciation for all members in the family included our extended family as

Joseph's headstone designed by Dad

Reverse side of Joseph's headstone

well. We lived in Colorado, but felt prompted to bury Joseph in Utah—so we held two funerals: one for friends and family in Colorado, and another for family in Utah. On the drive to Utah, the vehicle carrying Joseph's casket broke down. Without skipping a beat, our Dad's brother, JP, dropped everything he had going on to use one of his trucks and bring Joseph's body to Utah County. He didn't hesitate; he didn't give the inconvenience a second thought. Family was there to help whatever the cost. During this time, several other sacred experiences occurred with family members on both sides of the veil. Trial and affliction brought us together in a new way, and Joseph was the bridge. We would need these bonds as we increasingly felt prompted to begin a family mission, requiring us to unite and work together at an even deeper level.

Challenges can cause a family to unite and strengthen bonds of trust and love—essential if they are to work as a team to build the Kingdom of God.

Dealing with Grief

Dad didn't allow himself to wallow in grief. His kids needed him to show them an example of true Christianity under trial—to have faith and trust in God while walking through the valley of the shadow. Even though his heart was breaking, he continued to hold family scripture study and took time to have one-on-one conversations with each child who was ready. He shared insights that would offer context and understanding for why the Lord had taken our little brother. Dad didn't resist opening the photo albums, remembering the good times and the bad. Joseph's birthday was celebrated every year with some unique food or family activity. Talking through the events over the years, even repeatedly, ensured that Joseph was never forgotten in our memory, and it reaffirmed that death or other painful experiences are not to be feared. Pain has a purpose, and God was using it for *good* in our lives.

Visiting Joseph's plot at the Manti, Utah, cemetery, Dad would always encourage us to share memories of Joseph. We talked about his passing, read journal entries, and expressed our personal feelings.

Was it easy for Dad to take a deep breath, control his grief, and lead out in helping his family heal? Not at all. But ultimately, confronting the pain *with the Gospel* turned the dark experience for good. Instead of festering deep down—a sick wound that would only canker and destroy other weak areas in our lives— the heartrending wounds were allowed to heal. Dad channeled his heartbreak into investing more seriously into his children and helping us become a better family from the experience. Sometimes we wonder, "*Would things have been different if Dad had not been there?*" Would we have healed? Or would we have fallen apart? Thankfully, this trial helped our family become better, and it taught us that God has a purpose. We do not just endure—we *overcome*.

God is in the Details

In the book of Genesis, we learn that one of the meanings of the name Joseph is, "The Lord shall add to me another son."[4] Only three months after Joseph's passing, Mom gave birth to a baby boy. While the name 'Ezra Benson' had been suggested, both Dad and Mom felt impressed on the same day that the baby's name was to be Ephraim Joseph, and he happened to be born on Memorial Day. Even though Ephraim never knew Joseph in this life, he has always felt a special pride and connection to his brother that no doubt transcends this life. God truly did add to us another son.

When our parents were contemplating where to bury Joseph, the inspiration came to bury him in Manti, Utah. Some extended family members were confused with this choice. We had no relations living near Manti, nor did we have any ancestral

---

4   Genesis 30:24.

background there—so why Manti? Thankfully, our parents followed the Lord's guidance, and trusted Him for the rest. Eight years later, our family was prompted to purchase property about 15 minutes from Manti to build a homestead, with future plans for a home as well. Other family and friends have since moved to, or been found in this area, and it has become a second home to us. Who knew our family would be tied to the Sanpete Valley one future day? Only the Lord. If we had buried Joseph in Colorado, Idaho, or elsewhere in Utah, we would have been separated from his burial place, causing a wedge or divide that would have been difficult. Instead, the Lord inspired us to bury Joseph exactly where He knew we would eventually come so that our family could stay together.

What is the Purpose of Life?

Life is only a season. When we get to the other side, it will not matter how many trips we took, how many movies we watched, whether or not we had or completed a bucket list, etc. All that matters, when we face the Lord, is whether we bear the fruits of being *true* and *faithful*.

Joseph's passing taught us to invest our time and energy into lasting treasures—treasures we could carry into eternity.[5] Our trials caused us to develop greater reverence and devotion to God, thus we began making subtle adjustments to reflect the deeper feelings in our hearts. One day we were having family scripture study shortly after Joseph had passed, and Dad turned thoughtful. "I've been thinking we should start praying on our knees more often. Even during meal prayers, etc." We looked at each other. This was an interesting idea, but to be honest, there had been a new feeling of reverence in our home ever since Joseph's passing, and praying on our knees just seemed fittingly appropriate under the circumstances. Dad explained that kneeling was a sign of submission to God—a reflection of humility, reverence, and soberness. This physical gesture was really an outward demonstration of the change of heart

---

5   3 Nephi 13:19-21.

occurring within each of us and our family as a whole. So we began praying on our knees as a family—both at meals and morning and evening gatherings—and even during spontaneous prayers. We were learning to submit to God—to turn our family's aspirations over to Him, and to respect His authority and direction in a new way.

⁓

The Lord's work can only be done with clean hands and a pure heart. Trials can cause families to become purified, humble, and contrite—preparing them for a greater work.

⁓

The traumatic passing of Joseph prepared us for the next milestone in our family's life. The Lord had a specific mission for us as a family team, the vision of which would unfold in the months following Joseph's death.

CHAPTER
Four

BORN TO MAKE A DIFFERENCE

"Verily I say, men should be anxiously engaged in a good cause, and do many things of their own free will, and bring to pass much righteousness; For the power is in them, wherein they are agents unto themselves."

— *Doctrine & Covenants 58:27-28*

Every great home in scripture was led by a righteous patriarch with a vision given by God for that family. Abraham, Lehi, Nephi, Alma, Mormon, and countless other devoted fathers made significant sacrifices to gain that knowledge from God—and this principle is as true today as it was 2000 years ago. Where a father is not present—physically or emotionally/mentally—faithful mothers have filled this role.

From that eventful day in 1991, as Dad sat watching *America's Godly Heritage*, he knew he had a mission to fulfill, and each month—each year—brought additional puzzle pieces to light, painting a more complete picture. A vision does not emerge overnight—it is revealed line upon line, precept upon precept, according to our faith, dedication, and obedience.

In between changing diapers and making money to provide, Dad studied, researched, and gathered books on history, doctrine, science, and the arts. Some of us remember him sitting at one of those obnoxiously large computer monitors, typing away notes on the Book of Mormon paralleling our day, or perhaps making a catalog of good family movies. Dad began compiling his research on a simple, low-quality website—but at least it was a start! He taught in our local ward, he lived his faith in the workplace, and every conversation with friends and family would in some way or another turn to some important issue and the Lord's solution for it. No opportunity was lost! Dad was doing everything within his power—trusting that the Lord would reward his obedience with additional light and understanding. He researched scriptural solutions for pornography addiction, building relationships between fathers and sons, and structuring a Zion education curriculum. He also discovered compelling evidence for the lost tribes of Israel traveling to Europe. But *circulating* all of this knowledge weighed heavily on his mind— how could he get this information to the world?

"Produce Videos"

Direction came line upon line until the passing of little Joseph, when subsequent changes in our family's direction seemed to unleash new inspiration. Shortly before this tragedy, Dad felt the urge to publish books on building a Zion-like culture and parallels in the Book of Mormon with our present day. He had scarcely begun when trials and tribulations seemingly arose out of nowhere. Through perseverance, however, a few months after Joseph passed, clear instruction came: "Produce videos."

Produce videos?! Impossible! Dad had no background in film or graphics. He had never touched a professional camera before in his life. The only camera we owned was a simple camcorder. He was the father of a young family with six children ranging in age from infant to 10 years old. How was he supposed to take on film production? And where would he start?

But, characteristic of Dad, he didn't flinch. An investigation into various film schools quickly led him to determine that was *not* an option for him. The curriculum, even from schools that professed standards, was so degrading that Dad refused to risk his purity and place himself in a situation that may raise temptation. He had quit his stable job shortly after his mission because of immodest film covers, and there was no way he was going to compromise now either. Instead, he decided he would purchase training materials and teach himself from home—and he would restructure his children's homeschool curriculum to bring them along with him on the journey. Dad definitely always thought outside of the box!

⁓

An effective, lasting family mission is revealed by inspiration from the Lord.

⁓

Rethinking Our Approach

Too many good parents become inspired with a deep desire to do good, and then set their family to the side while chasing their own dreams. We know a mother who, a few years ago, was very active in conservative grassroots efforts and assisting liberty-minded candidates for public office. Meanwhile, her children spent their days sitting in government school classrooms, playing video games, or hanging out with friends, while she exhausted all of her energy and resources to save the Constitution. Sadly, every effort she made to turn the world around was literally being neutralized, undone, and reversed as her own next generation was being tutored by the opposition and disengaging from the battlefield. This mother tried bringing her daughters to a few events, but we remember watching them sitting in the back, slumped over their phones—their faces betraying just how bored and annoyed they really were. To this day, our friend is still busy trying to change the world—but her children are not united with her. The next generation was *lost*.

Our Dad never engaged in any cause, however small, without bringing his own children along. We can remember all looking at each other in surprise when we began attending the Book of

Eliza at the 2019 Book of Mormon Evidence Conference

Mormon Evidence Conferences a decade ago, and we couldn't find anyone else our age. Where were all the kids?

When Dad wanted to support a good cause, he brought his kids, or even sent us in his place to represent him and report back—whether for a grassroots political gathering or classes on first aid and self defense. When Dad was serving as a county delegate, we went to all the events. If he was meeting with an author or conservative thought leader, Dad brought some of his kids along. Whenever he was emailing or debating progressives on social media, we knew all the details and got the 'behind the scenes' for his written drafts. What about when Dad was called as Young Men's leader? Yes, even when we were only six or seven, the other leaders knew 'James' kids' would be tagging along to activities. On one occasion, some of the other leaders complained about this, but Dad was firm. If he was coming, they were coming. "They're so young!" the other leaders argued. "They'll be bored, rowdy, and distract you from serving our youth." Dad laughed and responded, "My kids will sit quietly, participate, and even help the older youth." And he was right! Kids can do *far* more than we think! Regrettably, we underestimate the abilities of our children.

Many Latter-day Saint parents never imagine that their *own* son or daughter could become one of the foreboding statistics of struggling youth. Many do not foresee or expect that their child will one day abandon the faith that was so carefully fostered from a young age. We have known so many fathers and mothers who "did everything right." They held Family Home Evening, enforced a rigorous curfew, followed every rule in the *For the Strength of Youth* pamphlet, and attended every Church meeting, youth activity, and Girls/Scout Camp. But when their children became teens or moved to college, everything seemed to fall apart— sometimes almost overnight. Apathy for the Gospel appeared— or worse—their children revolted against their upbringing. What happened? What was missing in the conversion process? While there will always be the exception—'Laman and Lemuel' youth— for many young people, apostasy and apathy are *unnecessary* tragedies. The missing ingredient was a family mission.

LEARNING TO APPRECIATE GOING WITH DAD

Hannah remembers: Dad took me to meetings with him when I was 12 years old or so. Dad had trained us from day one with discipline to sit quietly, be respectful, and *listen* when adults were having conversations. At first, I'll admit there were several times I was bored out of my mind. I had just finished all of my schoolwork and chores! I only had a few hours for play time—why was I being dragged off to listen as old men talked about . . . who knows what they were talking about! Most of it just went over my head. But talking back or rolling your eyes was unheard of at our house. It just didn't happen . . . not if you were smart, that is. I could stay home with extra chores, memorize verses, or miss an upcoming activity, or I could have a good attitude! So I'd bite my tongue and get in the car.

After a little while, I started making an effort to listen to the conversations going on around me. As we became more involved in our family documentary and research projects, I became more informed and interested in world events and issues. Curiously, I began paying attention to what I was hearing. Adventures at the United Nations trying to defend the family? Networking with non-Latter-day Saint scientists who were discovering evidence that validated the scriptures? Debates on gender roles? Answering *deep* faith crisis questions like Adam-God and polygamy? Hmmm, Dad was involving us in some pretty compelling conversations! I wanted to pay attention—and the more I listened, the more I learned, and the more excited I became. I was able to meet Elder Hartman Rector Jr., Rod Meldrum, Dr. Neil Flinders, Doug Brinley, Tim Ballard, Scott Bradley, Sharon Slater, Steve Smoot, former colleagues of President Ezra Taft Benson, directors of private schools, authors, musicians, and many, many others. This was the beginning of numerous associations that are essential in my work today. It all started with a Dad who made the sacrifices to make his kids the priority.

Our father taught us that the essential (but too often forgotten) ingredient to a faithful, joy-filled life is a cause—a consecrated mission directed by the Lord from day one. Testimonies are not gained through intellectual study, but by *doing*. Real faith is more than just a mere belief in ideals and scriptural facts—faith is action![1] Unless our children are fully immersed in the work, unless all their time and talents are consecrated selflessly—they will struggle to gain the faith, testimony, spirit, and power of the Gospel. A religion that does not require the sacrifice of all things—including our own ambitions and aspirations—does not have the power to save.[2]

For our family, this was why we homeschooled, and it was absolutely essential. It would have been impossible for Dad to perform the mission God gave our family without his team—his kids! The world literally became our classroom; engaging in real battlelines literally became our school. Our father gave us a family mission—and that mission changed our lives *forever*.

‿‿

Missions and causes should be approached with the understanding that your family is your team. Do good in the world with your family.

‿‿

---

1   *Lectures on Faith*, Lecture 7.

2   "Let us here observe, that a religion that does not require the sacrifice of all things never has power sufficient to produce the faith necessary unto life and salvation . . . It was through this sacrifice, and this only, that God has ordained that men should enjoy eternal life; and it is through the medium of the sacrifice of all earthly things that men do actually know that they are doing the things that are well pleasing in the sight of God. When a man has offered in sacrifice all that he has for the truth's sake, not even withholding his life, and believing before God that he has been called to make this sacrifice because he seeks to do his will, he does know, most assuredly, that God does and will accept his sacrifice and offering, and that he has not, nor will not seek his face in vain. Under these circumstances, then, he can obtain the faith necessary for him to lay hold on eternal life." *Lectures on Faith*, Lecture 6:7.

Ephraim, Mary, Ezra, & Eliza preparing for an expo with new banner displays

Sacrifice

No great work was ever achieved without struggle and sacrifice. The year 2005 was a rough year for our family, beginning with Joseph's passing. Dad's health began going downhill; he severely tore the ligaments in his left ankle—requiring the use of crutches; two-year-old Isaiah took an unexpected trip to the ER after his stomach mysteriously swelled up to six times its normal size; and various other problems seemed to rain down in fury upon our home—seemingly taunting us to give up such visionary dreams. As the famous quote goes, "I never said it would be easy, I only said it would be worth it." However, some days we wondered—would it *really* be worth it? When were we going to see some fruits?

During the summer, a new problem arose. Dad's software company, Agilent Technologies, closed his team down, and he realized he was about to lose his job. Taking a leap of faith, Dad

Dad's office at Agilent Technologies, 2006

still invested some of the funds we had into purchasing the film equipment we needed to begin movie production. Quoting from his journal around December 2005:

> Recently I have received several impressions to move and continue to move toward movie production and cameras. It was somewhat stressful purchasing the $4,000 Canon XL2 video camera, the digital camera, computer accessories, all when we are not going to have a job soon. . . . Ever since we started on the book and the movie production ideas all hell has broken loose. . . . My job is going away and has been far more stressful. . . . Nearly everyone believes that I am crazy to try this. The Lord has blessed us, however, that we have been able to make as much progress as we have through all of this. I know it is refining me as well, and I definitely need that!

Dad calculated that if our family sold everything and moved to a rental home for a year—combined with a severance pay from his former software job—we would have enough funds to work on documentaries for one year before our finances would run out. Through prayer, we felt this sacrifice was necessary. Heaven wasn't going to drop everything Dad needed right in his lap—he had to *work to make* the vision happen.

So, we moved. We were living in Loveland, Colorado, at the time—but we pulled up our roots, left the beautiful yard Dad designed and built with us—the elegant flagstone path, garden, backyard sandbox, flagpole, his beautiful handmade wooden gazebo, and the rose bushes—to move into a rental with an unfinished dirt yard with sagebrush in Saratoga Springs, Utah.

As Dad drove the truck from Colorado to Utah, we listened to *History of Joseph Smith by His Mother* on audiobook. He talked to us about why we were moving and all the good the Lord could accomplish if we were faithful and obedient. We could all sense that we were starting a new chapter in our lives—we would never be the same again. Dad knew he needed to produce three documentaries on the following subjects: the Book of Mormon parallels for our day, Darwinian evolution, and Zion education. But when these were finished, we weren't completely sure what would follow. We felt somewhat like Lehi, venturing into the wilderness, taking one step at a time. We didn't know where the road would lead.

"Family Projects" . . . Not "Dad's Projects"

From day one, Dad did not consider this new enterprise into video to be "Dad's projects." They were "family" projects. When he sat at his computer watching tutorials on Adobe Photoshop or video editing, we sat beside him and watched—99% of it going right over our heads. Nevertheless, we felt pretty important. We wanted to be like Dad! He was going to 'change the world'—though we weren't entirely sure what that meant—and so were we! Dad worked *with* us. He sacrificed hours and hours to build his family and train his children *through* this work.

In our free time, we children started making video slideshows and our own websites. Was it painfully obvious that kids had made them? Admittedly, yes, but Dad didn't seem to notice. He told us they were "great," gave suggestions, and even helped

Filming a scene in Nephites in Europe

us burn all of our slideshows onto our own DVD with his new computer. When we put the disc into our DVD player, it *actually* played on our TV. Wow, we felt *so* grown up!

Dad chose the name "ZionVision" for our family's new production company. If Dad was going to start a business, naturally, we followed suit. Nine-year-old James started Melting Pot, and then Mount Zion Productions, and 10-year-old Hannah created MHRL (a humorously long acronym for "My Heart Rejoices in the Lord," drawn from Hannah's song in 1 Samuel 2). Somehow, it made sense to her, but we were all relieved when she relinquished that name for something more . . . normal. We didn't know what we were going to do with these companies, but we wanted to be 'grown up' and we wanted to be like Dad.

When Dad began recording narration for his first documentary, *Creation and Evolution: A Witness of Prophets*, we were right by his side, creating a makeshift audio studio out of red and blue sleeping bags clamped to 10-foot mobile poles in our living room, creating a small area to eliminate echoes in the recording. Every time someone came over to narrate a scripture or a prophetic statement for the documentary, we set up our makeshift 'audio studio' with poles and blankets. When recording was done, we took the stands down so we could have a family living room again. Our 'office' was a little room next to the kids' bedroom. Every morning when we rolled out of bed, we could hear Dad's fingers flying across the keyboard. Our brother James helped Dad with the DVD rendering, menus, and equipment while filming, and Hannah was assigned to Photoshop. To this day, one of the cartoon pictures Hannah helped Dad create in the *Creation and Evolution* documentary still bears a hidden 'Easter egg' that marks the 'Dad and kids' team. The scene has her nickname written in cursive in the corner: "Peps." Dad *never* worked on any project, wrote any article, researched any subject, made any video, or visited with any influential friend, without one or more of his kids right by his side. We cannot emphasize this enough.

AUDIO EDITING WITH DAD

Leah remembers: While working on the movie *Creation and Evolution: A Witness of Prophets*, I remember at eight years old, Dad asking me if I would like to edit audio with him. I said yes, excited to be part of the 'big project.' Dad handed me a pair of professional headphones—headphones I knew cost a couple hundred dollars. I reverently put the headphones on and watched as Dad imported and edited audio narration files. After about 10 minutes, my head was practically swimming with phrases repeated over and over. But it was just another example of Dad involving us in the projects. Dad also had me draw images of Noah's ark and the Second Coming (he gave me a descriptive lesson on how to draw fire), which he included *in* the movie. Dad didn't wait for kids to be 'old enough' to involve them. He came up with creative ideas to help us be a part of the projects.

*Mary started learning computer programming and proudly got a
matching "data nerd" shirt with Dad*

Changing the World Through the Family

One day, Dad was praying for help. How could he best assist in
bringing clarity and hope amidst all the confusion in the world?
The words came to his mind, *"I am the way!"* So simple! Jesus
Christ is literally the answer and His way is not complicated. But
then Dad pondered why everyone has a different interpretation of
the Lord's doctrine, lifestyle, and will! How can we know the true
Son of God? The answer came: *"I have sent My servant Joseph
Smith."* Suddenly, Dad felt the power of the Restoration message
in a new way. "How could our family help?" he asked. Again, a
gentle response was given: *"Feed My sheep."* The answers are not
in programs, fads, influencers, or the latest bestselling books. The
answers are in the revelations of God, in scripture, and through

Joseph Smith—including all faithful and inspired men and women who have echoed his message since.[3]

Through prayer and hours of pondering, our family felt impressed that our mission was to promote Joseph Smith's vision and teachings for building Zion. This would be done through four primary means: upholding scripture, defending the Prophet Joseph Smith and his doctrine, restoring a pure culture, and mobilizing and equipping families to take on their own mission. Application of this principle may look different for some. If there is no father or mother to lead out, a sibling, uncle, aunt, cousin, or grandparent can unite their family in changing the world.

Proverbs 29:18 reads, "Where there is no vision, the people perish . . ." This is true for every family. Where there is no family vision, family cause, and family mission, that family will 'perish'—meaning, the values, culture, identity and purpose of that particular family will not survive to future generations. The legacy will be lost because the children are disengaged and disconnected from their forefathers. They may have fun together, but there is no united cause or effort that gives them a family identity and purpose.

Families were meant for more than holiday dinners and recreational vacations. They were purposely designed by God to work *together* in a beautiful symphony, creating a dynamic masterpiece. Each child was sent in a specific order with unique talents, personality traits, and dreams to work together with the rest of the family. Your family is your team. Do not set them aside and chase after strangers. Do good in the world with your family—the team God personally set up for a *reason*!

United we stand, divided we fall. Today, the voice of truth is being stifled and suppressed, but when family choruses begin proclaiming truth throughout the world, that voice will never be silenced. Truth and light will defeat the darkness.

---

3   ". . . give heed unto all his [Joseph Smith's] words and commandments . . . For by doing these things the gates of hell shall not prevail against you; yea, and the Lord God will disperse the powers of darkness from before you, and cause the heavens to shake for your good, and his name's glory." Doctrine & Covenants 21:4, 6.

CHAPTER
Five

"TOUCH THESE STONES"

*". . . [H]ow is it that ye have forgotten that the Lord is able
to do all things according to his will, for the children of
men, if it so be that they exercise faith in him?
Wherefore, let us be faithful to him."*

— *1 Nephi 7:12*

Shortly after Dad started ZionVision (later the Joseph Smith Foundation), he prayed one night that the Lord would "touch these stones." Just as the Brother of Jared petitioned that his gathered stones would be magnified by the Lord,[1] in like manner, our family had collected our own 'stones': we made the necessary monetary sacrifices, we purchased the cameras and equipment, and we invested in training to produce documentaries from our home. Despite our best efforts, we knew it was not enough. We were too weak, too frail, too poor, and too ignorant. We tried to be obedient, we tried to be diligent, and now Dad was bringing our 'stones' to the Lord, humbly requesting divine aid in bringing light to the whole world.

Leah and Hannah can distinctly remember one warm day in August 2006 when we came home from a fun activity to find Dad, in the office, ecstatic. He had stayed at home, working long hours cooped up in the little bedroom, trying to create

---

1 Ether 3:1-6.

his very first animation in Adobe After Effects. The first project he undertook was the ZionVision logo opener. It was a full-on animation with electric static fusing together the words, "FAITH," "FAMILY," "EDUCATION," and "TECHNOLOGY" into the title, "ZIONVISION." It was his very first project and he finished the entire animation in *one* day. Very impressive for a beginner! We were stunned, but no one more so than Dad. For years afterward, every time he looked at it, he would remark, "I still don't know how I did that. How on earth did that happen?"

"Purification Projects"

Hannah has always called our family projects "purification projects" because they have refined, tested, and chastened us in ways we never thought possible. We literally could not make progress on a documentary or book if we were being slothful or contentious as a family. We had a choice—repent and succeed, or remain where we were and fail. Sometimes we failed; sometimes we succeeded. Sometimes we were all on board and united; at other times, some family members were stronger, and, like Nephi building the ship, rallied the weak to stand firm and believe that the Lord could accomplish all things if we exercised faith in Him. We had to turn to the Lord for help, or nothing could be done. God had to intervene, cleanse our home, and cause us to grow. As the Lord told the Prophet Joseph Smith:

 . . . to all those who have desires to bring forth and establish this work; And no one can assist in this work except he shall be humble and full of love, having faith, hope, and charity, being temperate in all things, whatsoever shall be entrusted to his care. (Doctrine & Covenants 12:7-8)

God's work must be done with clean hands and a pure heart.

Some days our family struggled. On February 28, 2006, Dad recorded in his journal, "the buddies [Dad's term for his kids] were unruly and we have had a difficult time keeping the Spirit in the home." Soberly, Dad added, "I should have gathered everyone for prayer more often. May the Lord give us the strength to keep moving forward." One month later, along similar lines, he wrote: "Hopefully we can become more humble, patient and filled with love—we need it to do this work. The Lord will support those who trust in Him."

Dad reminded us of scriptural promises—that if we were faithful, the Lord would intervene when we needed help. We all remember Dad telling us a story from his mission, when he and a companion were accidentally locked out of their apartment. They had begun baking fish sticks in the oven and stepped out for a moment, only to find the door locked when they returned. Their keys were inside. Dad and his companion yanked on the door, tried every innovation they could think of, and even tried to call someone to open the door. But two hours later, no help had arrived. Dad and his companion were panicking about the apartment catching on fire from the fish sticks in the oven—no doubt black cinders by this point.

Exhausted, they sat down in their car and suddenly Dad's companion turned to him and said, "Elder Stoddard, you always do the right thing and always follow the rules. Why don't you just pray and open the door?" Oh wow, talk about pressure! With that encouragement, Dad felt prompted to exert faith and plead for help. Then they returned to the apartment and pushed on the door. To their astonishment, it swung wide open. The same door they had been banging and shaking just a little while before! Rushing to the oven, they opened the door and, lo and behold, their fish sticks were not burned and in perfect condition. Stunned, they sat down and ate their dinner. This and other stories would come to mind when we hit our own roadblocks, inspiring us to persevere and rely on the Lord.

Miracles During Documentary Production

As our family endeavored to be obedient, through the sunshine and the rain, the Lord did not abandon us!

IMPOSSIBLE MUSIC SCORING DEADLINE

Hannah remembers: I want to share one quick miracle from the 'behind the scenes' of *Unlocking the Mystery of the Two Prophets*. Honestly, there are so many stories behind all of the videos, and I think those providential moments are important to remember and retell because every family and individual with a mission can often become discouraged. It is easy to grow weary! We can all relate to Andrew van der Bijl—the man who smuggled Bibles behind the Iron Curtain into Communist countries and the author of *God's Smuggler*—who hit his own rock bottom when he first began. In one interview, he said: "I was often at the point of giving up. But I think I decided that whatever happens, my life is not my own. I have to stick to my decision. I will follow Jesus! Sometimes I would physically hang on to my bed and say, 'Lord, but I want to continue following you!'" With that said, miracles are REAL! This is one miracle of many.

To edit the 'Two Prophets' video, we only had one month from the day we shot the first interview to the deadline. This meant we only had around 3-4 days to complete the music (we generally have 3-4 weeks). The bulk of the work was done on a two day sprint. The first day, we dug in and worked hard—*really* hard! Despite many tender mercies, we were hammered and discouraged when night came. Reality was staring us in the face. There was *no way* we were going to have this video scored by the deadline, which meant many sections would be dry and devoid of any music. As I looked over the transcript late that night, my heart broke. I had begun to sense why this message was important and I wanted so badly for the video to be done well. And yet . . . I was watching those hopes sink. I went to bed that night pleading with God to break up the feeling of despair and help me to be content with whatever He intended for this video.

The next morning, I was literally afraid to go back to work—from a fear of failure—but we began again. Miracles unfolded! One of the highlights came that morning as a new piece of music was dropped into our lap minutes before we had to score an important climax of the video. At first, we had no musical pieces that would work. Suddenly—out of nowhere—the perfect piece appeared! The timing was perfect . . . the crescendos were perfect, the instruments came in at the right time! It was made in heaven!! I cried out tears of thanksgiving as the section came together, and before the day was over, many other sections were completed. We finished the entire documentary on time and on schedule.

There is NO WAY we could have done this on our own, but as I have often thought, "The Lord wants the Gospel taught more than we do, so TRUST Him. He will give the strength and the means to accomplish the vision He inspired."

BREAKTHROUGH WHEN ANIMATING STATUES

Leah remembers: While working on the Two Prophets video, my responsibility was creating the animations and adding sound effects. Sometimes, money played a factor in the quality of those animations. There were specific pieces of add-on equipment, called 'plugins,' that could be used to animate in the software I was using (Adobe After Effects), but they cost about $250-$300 each. As money doesn't grow on trees, buying expensive plugins merely to add extra flare to the videos wasn't an option. I learned to work around some of the design issues with free options.

One day, however, Hannah came to me with an exciting idea: she wanted the two statues of Joseph and Hyrum Smith in the Salt Lake Temple niches to "build" themselves out of particles. I thought that was a cool idea, but immediately my mind began wondering *how* it could actually be done with the tools that I had.

After about 3+ hours of research, I came back with the verdict. Hannah was sitting in an office chair across the room and I swung around to face her. According to reviews by After Effects animators and experts, and my own personal experimentation, there was no way to create self-building particle statues without a $300 plugin. Hannah listened, but was not discouraged. Cheerfully she said, "There has to be a way with the free tools. Find it!" At this point I was slightly annoyed because, despite my own hopes, it really didn't seem feasible, and Hannah just wasn't seeing the unreasonableness of her request. Experts much smarter than me had said it couldn't be done!

Then Hannah added, "I bet if you pray about it, the Lord can make it happen." She also mentioned the story of Nephi building the ship. I paused and thought for a minute. It seemed like a very good idea . . . *in theory*. I stared at my laptop screen wondering how exactly I was going to make something from nothing. But I got on my knees, took a leap of faith, and prayed that God would show me how it was supposed to work. I prayed, like Nephi, that He would show me the right tools to use so I could make the design, and that I wouldn't doubt. Then I got to work.

I started dragging and dropping bubble effects, changing parameters, shrinking the bubbles and adding track mattes, not really knowing what I was doing. There was no method or tutorial. About 16 hours of work later, I had a small stream of bubbles that looked like particles swirling up, creating a statue of Joseph Smith, which I then duplicated and tweaked for Hyrum. I was ecstatic!

All the kids working together in the office

God had done it! I was looking at particle-building statues made from bubbles! The almost frightening thing was that I had no idea how I had done it. I had been twirling options on and off and adjusting parameters, a method which usually results in chaos. And, as I didn't believe in random chance evolution, this could only be the act of an intelligent designer—and it wasn't me.

To this day—and with the additional skills I have learned—I still have no idea how to create bubble-building statues based on my own skills. I tried replicating the process later, but wasn't able to. It was nothing short of a pure miracle, a testimony that the Lord wants His work done.

OVERCOMING WEAKNESSES & NATURAL INABILITY, WEAK THINGS BECOME STRONG

Hannah remembers: When I was 14 years old. I participated in a research project and also began taking courses to study web development, audio and video editing, digital photography, and so forth. When some parents have commented to me that their own children struggle to learn some of these skills, I completely understand where they are coming from! I know some children who are gifted, but for most of us, myself included, we could not gain these skills on our own strength. I remember writing in my journal, March 12, 2009, when I was 14 years old: "Today God helped me with my HTML training. I was able to learn more quickly. It was like my mind was opened." This is another entry a few years later: "I have received a lot of help from God in terms of code problems. Several times I got the right answer, received ideas and found potential problems in a way that really made the problems easier to fix."

Being dependent on the Lord helped motivate me to be obedient and keep my standards high so I was 'standing in holy places' when needs arose. Honestly, having a family mission is probably what saved me spiritually from rebelling or taking the wrong path in life. Being engaged in this cause kept me focused, drove me to my knees, and helped convert me—no longer allowing my stubborn and headstrong nature to overcome the good desires of my heart.

I feel our family was purposely given assignments that were above and beyond our ability in order for us to remain humble and recognize our complete *dependence* on Him, instead of relying on the arm of flesh. My insecurity and lack of natural abilities drove me to rely on God. Growing up, I was often sick with strange symptoms from some kind of chronic illness that could lay me sick in bed for days with migraines, and in my mid-teen years, I noticed I was struggling with brain fog. I remember waking up early, before anyone else in the house, so I could memorize poetry and scripture to try sharpening my mental skills, or feeling frustrated with myself when I couldn't remember details or struggled to grasp certain concepts. These physical weaknesses taught me to pray, because I realized that accomplishing this work was impossible on my own. I cannot count the number of times as I grew older that I would be on the radio or in the middle of an interview, and inspiration would come, helping me communicate and relay the material I needed to share.

One other brief story: we were working on a trailer for one of our documentary films, but Dad was busy with a big work project, so I was left to take the lead. I remember sitting in our office in Saratoga Springs and sweating bullets. I had *no* idea what I was doing, and I didn't want to fail because I was doing this for the Lord and didn't want to offer Him a mud hut instead of a temple. I remember closing the door and getting on my knees. I prayed for several minutes, begging the Lord to teach me and show me what to do because I didn't know where to start. I got up and sat at the computer for a few minutes. Suddenly, ideas began coming! I was impressed with certain video editing principles and direction on where to go to learn more. I believe we completed that trailer within a few days to a week. Later, I was listening to a professional video editor, and he began listing principles for producing video trailers. I started laughing because he shared some of the same concepts that had been brought to my mind earlier! This experience reminded me that our God is not *just* the King of the Universe. He is a perfect, complete man with a fully developed character and personality. He is the perfect scientist, the perfect artist, the perfect musician, the perfect poet, the perfect chef, the perfect fashion designer, the perfect humorist, the perfect writer, the perfect gardener, the perfect parent, the perfect engineer, and so forth. God is trying to help us develop our character and personality to become like Him and He can help us in any setting, at any time, with any topic!

Struggles test our endurance and faith. How committed are we to see God's will accomplished, and will we give in or overcome through Christ? If you think you are going to do it on your own strength, with your own talents, your own innovation and creativity, I have news for you! You are going to fail. Without Him, you will not succeed. With Him, you *cannot* fail.

Only God Can

Growing up, Dad gave us a guideline in dating and relationships that remains true for all of this work. Dad would remind us that none of us are perfect, we all have weaknesses that require patience, love, and support. However, there are three foundational characteristics that are non-negotiable:

- Honesty & integrity
- Consecration to serve God and engage in His work
- Discipline to sacrifice appetite & follow the Lord's standards

Dad focused on these three attributes when we were being raised. Dad understood that God can work miracles and overcome all other obstacles through His strength. There will be no hindrance to help you progress. You may struggle with being unorganized, or impatient, or light-minded, or oversensitive, or resentful—but if you are honest, if you daily lay down your life to do God's work, and if you are willing to give up any appetite to live high standards (media, food, entertainment, etc.), the Lord can do the rest! You will not be held back. He will refine and grant you a change of heart until you are born of God.

Years later, one of us received a blessing wherein they were counseled to be content with limitations the Lord gives when guiding a family mission. One day, these obstacles will stand as a witness that God's work is never truly accomplished through our weak, mortal strength. It is only God who makes all things possible to resolve the challenge that lays before us. If we serve Him with obedience and sincerity, miracles will come—this is our family testimony.

CHAPTER
Six

LOSE YOUR LIFE . . . TO SAVE IT

"Love to be real, it must cost—it must hurt—
it must empty us of self."

— *Mother Teresa*

In 2007, we finished our first documentary, *Creation and Evolution: A Witness of Prophets*. We couldn't believe it was real—we had just made a movie! Now it was sitting in our hands. For Dad, we can only imagine the joy he must have felt. He had received an assignment, and step one was now finished! Some time later, Dad recorded in his journal, "Last night we were watching the Creation video on our new HD TV and I was struck with the blessing that was given in completing that work despite our lack of experience. It is almost unbelievable."

Learning to Take Responsibility as Kids

However, our savings were now gone, and Dad had to return to work. After teaching for one year at a private school, he found a full-time job as a software engineer. Now the only time he had for our family projects was at night, on weekends, and during holidays. Progress now depended on us kids. Could we take up the mantle and keep the work going, even while Dad was away? At this time, Hannah was 14, James almost 13, and Leah, 11.

Dad would assign us tutorials and then specific tasks to complete while he was gone. As much as Dad loved us, he knew that if he tolerated slothfulness, disobedience, or irresponsibility we would bear miserable consequences when we became adults—so he required the tasks to be completed when he got home without exception.

Dad looked to scripture and the words of inspired prophets for guidance in how to 'parent,' and he recognized that the Lord held a high standard when it came to work ethic. Dad was strict on us fulfilling commitments. Sadly, this ideal is lacking in many homes today. Parents do not require their sons and daughters to be disciplined. You have to ask a child two, three, maybe even four times before they will respond! While this attitude may appear 'loving,' it sets children up for failure and causes chaos in the home. We were also expected to come immediately when called.

⌒

"True education trains in self-denial and self-mastery.
True education regulates the temper, subdues passion and
makes obedience to social laws and moral order a guiding
principle of life." [1] — *President David O. McKay*

⌒

Although it was hard, we are all very grateful that Dad did not tolerate idleness and disobedience. We were raised early to become men and women who *accomplished* goals competently, instead of only dreaming about them. Trust us—we were far from perfect, and it took a lot of patience! Some assignments we utterly failed or had to start over again and again from scratch.

Dad would assign us smaller tasks that he would then put together to create a masterpiece on the weekend: research this quote, design this graphic, or create this animation. He would call at lunch to see how we were doing and check up on the job status. He would also ask how things were proceeding at home—if everything was

---

1   David O. McKay, in *Conference Report*, April 1928, 102.

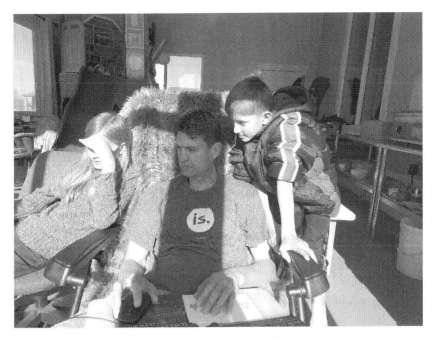

Researching with Mary & Ezra

running smoothly or descending into chaos! When his colleagues overheard his phone conversations, they jokingly quipped: "What are you doing over there? Running a sweatshop?"

All the same, they knew Dad loved his kids more than anything. Once or twice when Dad took us to his work, we were surprised that all of his work buddies knew exactly who we were. To know Dad was to know his love for his children. Even when we lived in Colorado, Dad would bring Hannah (age 10), James (age 8), and Leah (age 7) to his work on 'Bring-Your-Kids-To-Work-Day.' Leah still remembers drawing chameleons there with Dad.

The Secret to Motivating Children

At 6:00 a.m., our alarms would ring, and we would head down to the office to complete our personal scripture study, our school work for the day, and Dad's assigned projects. Some days, we were on fire—we charged into that room excited and confident—we were going to change the world! On others we woke up tired, irritated, and lazy—the 'fun' was gone, and all we saw was a lot of work—while our peers were chasing around the neighborhood with cellphones and friends. Our lives were nothing like a dramatic movie with heroic characters and an epic soundtrack. Walking downstairs, turning on the computers, and pulling up a documentary that seemed to stretch out for weeks with no end in sight was the last thing we *wanted* to do. It was often tempting to roll our eyes and laugh when JSF (Joseph Smith Foundation) fans would tell us how "talented" and "smart" we were. We lived a different reality: these documentaries came about through incredible miracles and a lot of blood, sweat, and even tears.

Most days we remembered *why* we were doing this. There were men and women who were suffering, and we were going to help them! Dad had us watch movies on history, Communism, social conflicts, science, and many other 'battlelines' facing us in the twenty-first century to help us 'catch the vision.' Every dinner table conversation centered around important issues and doctrine. Dad took us to meet the faces of those who were hurting—face to face—whether we were visiting another family or helping someone one on one. He didn't sanitize or whitewash our understanding of pain in the world. We knew details about torture methods in North Korea, emotional trauma following an abortion, and the reality of how hard life was outside our door so we had a visual reminder of *why* we were making sacrifices.

But some days, we honestly didn't really care about the war between good and evil, light and darkness. Perhaps we did care, but we were just too tired to keep working and miss out on "fun" things. We were still young, and we didn't have the wisdom that time and experience brings. Sometimes, we just didn't want to work. Dad communicating the cause to us was not enough. We had to not only embrace the mission, but learn to lay down our lives and sacrifice to accomplish it. We had to learn to care for others, more than we cared for ourselves. We had to *love*.

∽

*The two greatest commandments—love for God and love
for their fellowman—should be the driving motivation
of our children's careers, school, and life.*

∽

Zeal for "truth" may last for a little while, but when adversity comes, if our roots are not deeply grounded, we will wither in the sweltering summer heat. Children need a purpose and motivation that reaches far outside of themselves—they need to focus *out*, not *in*. Dad drew a life philosophy from the scriptures that could be summarized in four letters: LOVE. It was this simple:

1. The world is dying and starving for help.
2. Joy does not come from living for yourself.
3. You have been given privileges that others do not have. You have a duty to lift others and you will one day stand before God and be held accountable for what you did and did not do.

Mother Teresa

To help us gain compassion, our Dad intentionally *showed* us suffering—the reality of human struggle—from the safety of our home. The first way he did this was through film—particularly two motion pictures on the life of Mother Teresa. With visuals, music, and dialogue, these films showed us in a safe and non-traumatic way the reality of suffering in the world: men, women, and children who were rummaging through mounds of trash just to find scraps for their next meal, and sleeping amongst filth and disease, only to curl up in a corner, forgotten and alone—breathing their last without love or hope to comfort them.

Mother Teresa (1910-1997) was a Catholic nun who gave up her privileged position as headmistress of a school in Calcutta, India, to live a life of labor and exhaustion in the slums to bring relief to the suffering. The movies *Mother Teresa: In the Name* of *God's Poor* (1997) and *Mother Teresa* (2003) were powerful and moving. Our family watched them multiple times, carefully analyzing many scenes. We saw a vivid testimony that real love *hurts*—that it takes inconvenient sacrifice to make a difference. Dad would say:

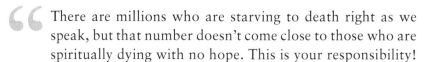

> There are millions who are starving to death right as we speak, but that number doesn't come close to those who are spiritually dying with no hope. This is your responsibility!
>
> Your life is not your own. You have been given so many opportunities, you have a duty to wear out your life helping others. You might not go to a third world country; you may spend your days spiritually saving souls. Either way, your life should be consecrated to helping others. That is where true happiness comes from.

To ensure that our children remain loyal and committed means more than enlisting them in the war. If we simply talk about a cause, the work remains self centered. If a child's accomplishments become the cause, everything becomes about *them—their* battle, *their* heroism, and *their* talents. They become the hero, and pride becomes the driving motivation. This mistake can sometimes cause the downfall of some young men and women who go on two-year missions for the Church. Are they really there for the Lord? Or are they there for their image along with expectations from their family and culture? For our children to succeed, they need to serve out of selfless love.

Watching Dad's Example

No child respects a parent or mentor who does not live what they preach. As President David O. McKay well said:

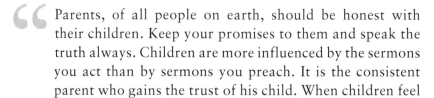

> Parents, of all people on earth, should be honest with their children. Keep your promises to them and speak the truth always. Children are more influenced by the sermons you act than by sermons you preach. It is the consistent parent who gains the trust of his child. When children feel

Shipping Faith Crisis 1 with Ephraim, Eliza, & a friend

that you reciprocate their trust, they will not violate your confidence nor bring dishonor to your name.[2]

In our home, Dad's lifestyle was *paramount* in determining if we as children would accept or reject this "love lifestyle." In order for the Joseph Smith Foundation to come about, Dad paid the greatest price. It wasn't as though he was a retired, wealthy man without a life. It wasn't as though God dropped the Joseph Smith Foundation in his lap, and he had fun running it on the weekends. He was a father of nine living children. He worked full time trying to provide. He had chronic health issues (likely cancer) for around two decades that meant every day brought some kind of pain somewhere. He had severe insomnia, and he inherited generational nerve issues. He had Church callings and he was diligent in his home teaching. There were so many hobbies he would have preferred to invest in any day. Not to mention the strain from enduring criticism leveled against him (on levels many people never experience) by mockers who thought he was a 'dreamer.' It took hours of daily prayer, inspiration, continual repentance and *many* miracles to push through. He did it out of love—love for God and love for others.

<hr>

2   David O. McKay, in *Conference Report*, April 1955, 26-27.

Dad didn't invent this idea of sacrifice on his own. Not only did he draw examples from the scriptures, but he was raised in a home where he saw this kind of love firsthand. Year after year, we saw his parents—our grandparents—serve time and time again. When our excavator thumb broke, and we needed it for our homestead, Grandpa came down from Idaho, suited up in 100 degree weather, and welded it back on for us. While others were retired and vacationing, he and Grandma continued working as truck drivers for *years* beyond the normal age range, and whenever Dad or one of his siblings needed help or had a new baby, Grandma was always there to clean, cook, and tend children. She was continually giving aid, encouragement, support, and sacrificing her time to serve. Dad always called Grandma, "a modern day John Tanner."[3] The simple fact is: the Joseph Smith Foundation and our family would not exist if it were not for this labor of love. Dad was simply carrying on this legacy.

---

3   John Tanner was an early Church member who converted to the Gospel after his diseased leg was miraculously healed. In December 1838, after receiving an impression to "go immediately to the Church," John sold all his property and traveled 500 miles to Kirtland. At this time, the Church was in serious financial trouble and the Kirtland Temple was about to be destroyed because the mortgage payment was past due. Upon arriving, John paid the $2,000 mortgage as a loan for the temple. He also donated $43,000 to the Church.

His fortune now gone, John (also known as "Father" Tanner) followed the Saints to Missouri, where he and his family experienced heavy persecution and starvation. In 1844, he was called on a mission to the Eastern States. Before leaving, John visited Joseph Smith in Nauvoo and returned the bank note for the $2,000. The Prophet, not understanding, asked John what he would like him to do with the note. Father Tanner replied, "Brother Joseph, you are welcome to it." The Prophet then laid his right hand upon Father Tanner's shoulder and said, "God bless you, Father Tanner. Your children shall never beg for bread." This prophecy was fulfilled, and John Tanner's children and descendants have never begged for bread.

John Tanner's story is depicted in the film *Treasure in Heaven: The John Tanner Story* by T. C. Christensen.

"WE DON'T ASK, 'WHAT DO I WANT TO DO?'"

Hannah remembers: Dad always made it a priority to make sure we lived in clean and safe neighborhoods, and he ensured that he made enough money to support that. We never lacked for the best food, clothing and everything else we really needed. However, I can remember periods of financial strain. I knew from overhearing my parents talk about how to make ends meet to keep the Joseph Smith Foundation going, that if it hadn't been for miracles and my Grandma Stoddard's generous help, we wouldn't have made it through. On top of it all, I can remember from a young age watching my Dad struggle through pain. I remember watching scenes of William Wilberforce's pain in *Amazing Grace: The Story of William Wilberforce* in 2015 and thinking, "Ugh. This is too real. I have seen this in real life." I can remember Dad once saying that he was driven by the recurring thought that every moment he wasted would cost someone blood or suffering in the future. Every moment he served, however, could spare someone that pain. That is what made it worth it to him.

One night, I came home and saw my Dad sprawled out on the floor in our living room. He looked exhausted, and I could tell he hadn't showered after a long day at work. Going up to him I said, "Hey Dad! Tonight don't think about anything you are supposed to do. Just think about what *you* want to do!" Quietly, he opened his eyes and said, "I never ask that question. My life isn't about what I want, but what the Lord wants done." I never forgot that moment, nor the living example he gave of laying his life down for others. This consecration did not mean we never had rest and relaxation. We loved (and still love) playing basketball together, opening our home to friends and guests, or enjoying a clean uplifting movie. But everything we did was calculated to do good and rejuvenate ourselves to better serve! I am immeasurably grateful for those lessons.

NO RESPECTER OF PERSONS

Leah remembers: Dad treated everyone he knew with compassion. His trust level varied depending on the character of the individual, but he always looked out for and helped everyone. He wasn't a "respecter of persons."

He had compassion and consideration for everyone he met, regardless of age, position, race, gender, or background. There was no agenda or ulterior motive. It didn't matter if it was a grandmother at a Book of Mormon conference needing help with her son who was leaving the Church, or the kids in my Sunday School class (young teens loved him). This attitude of love built my confidence that he would treat me the same way, and he did.

There was no mask, no airs, no prestige, no position—just a humble sort of humility and understanding that drew people to him. At the last Book of Mormon Evidence conference our family attended, a lady came up to us and said that she was so sorry to hear Dad had passed. She said she only attended the conferences to talk to him because she felt like he truly cared.

SACRIFICING TO HELP THOSE IN NEED

Mary remembers: I remember Dad always giving up so much to help people. There would be times when he would come home after a long hard day of working and he would be exhausted, but he still kept going. He would talk to people for hours trying to help them with different questions they had or things that they were struggling with even on the days when he was suffering from really bad health problems.

*Dad holding a role play class on effective communication &
constructive, civil debate*

There was one day when it was hard for him to even talk without it causing him pain, but he still had people over because they needed help. That night, after the visitors left, I remember him sitting there in pain, and he couldn't sleep because he was hurting so bad. Instead of thinking about himself and what he would like to do, he sat there talking about the things that this person was going through and what could be done to help other people who were going through the same things—whether it was to write an article, make a podcast, or something else.

Other times, he would work on writing articles, editing books, or anything that needed to be done for the projects. He never did anything because he wanted to or because it would help him; everything he did was to help others or to serve God.

First Step: Real Love at Home

Dad first taught us this principle in the home. We learned to quietly lay down our life for our siblings—without worldly praise, without accolades, without 'likes' on social media. We didn't win an award for helping our little brother with his schoolwork, or changing that diaper, or cleaning the kitchen, or staying up late with our little sister who was sick. While we could receive praise for producing documentaries or books through the Joseph Smith Foundation, our real test of character and love came behind closed doors at home, with no one watching and just a little sibling in need who may not be able to return the favor. Home is where it all began.

Teach children to willingly serve and love their brothers and sisters. The home is their greatest, and most difficult, work.

Second Step: Helping the World

The sad truth is that most children today are *not taught* to have empathy. In the Doctrine and Covenants, we learn that when 24 years old, Joseph Smith was literally *weeping* for Zion, for the men and women who didn't have access to the Book of Mormon and Gospel truths. How many of us weep? How many of our children wake up each morning feeling heavy because Christians are persecuted in other countries? How many pray with anxiety for fellow teens who are addicted to pornography? How many express urgency to use their time well because babies are being aborted, millennials are leaving the Church, marriages are falling apart, young girls take pill after pill to bury their depression and anxiety, and young men are drowning their loneliness and indolence in video games?

Eliza squeezing lemons

Anyone can bake cookies and mow a neighbor's lawn, but real love *hurts*. Cookies are nice and the lawn does need to be cared for, but if we stop there, we have left the world where it is today—broken and hopeless. Real love is sacrifice. It is surrendering your comfort, your dreams, your wants, and your desires to bring hope to another without any personal reward or return.

It was hard producing *For Our Day: Covenant on the Land*; Leah and Hannah gave up a lot of fun activities to finish *Hidden Bloodlines*; we pulled a few all-nighters to finish *For Our Day: Divinely Sanctioned Governments*. Well, actually we pulled a few all-nighters with almost every project (and may or may not have gotten a little cranky), but it was worth it! Tears were shed over the book *Faith Crisis 2: Behind Closed Doors*; and some mornings when finishing *Unlocking the Mystery of the Two Prophets*, we woke up filled with insecurity and a lack of confidence in our own ability, and for good reason. It took grit, determination, prayer, and disciplined will power—the will to act—to push through the roadblocks and finish.

When we worked long days in the office even while sick, when we skipped a fun activity because someone needed us to comfort them, when we studied computer skills we weren't really interested in or were hard to understand, we didn't do it because we were 'saints'—we were pretty headstrong kids. We did it because there were men and women we had never met personally who needed our help, and we had been taught to *love* them. Doing this took a lot of faith—faith we didn't have at first but learned to earn and grow. Real love—the sacrificial, long-suffering and patient love—is hard. It tears you apart, and requires you to lay down your dreams, but this is the only love that makes an effective difference in the world for good.

⁓

True love is willing to sacrifice,
without reward or return.

⁓

Joy vs. Pleasure

Sometimes when we talk about living a life of sacrifice—"losing our life to save it"—people seem to imagine the path of discipleship will leave them in misery. They imagine God as a controlling dictator who will tear away everything they love, will destroy all their dreams leaving them to spend the rest of their lives employed in the most menial, hateful tasks—all in the name of 'sacrifice.' While this may seem slightly hyperbolic, do we sometimes think—and in turn, *act*—this way? The Prophet Joseph Smith taught:

"" Happiness is the *object* and *design* of our existence; and will be the end thereof, if we pursue the path that leads to it; and this path is virtue, uprightness, faithfulness, holiness, and keeping ALL the commandments of God.[4]

The world would have us believe that to live a sacrificial Christian life is to live a colorless, boring, or even painful existence—while those who live for themselves lead happy, adventurous, and comfortable lives. Ironically, when you dig beneath deceptive exteriors, not everything is as it appears. It's an interesting paradox: a mirage that can only last for so long. Instead, our experience has taught us the scriptural truth that living to serve someone else is the secret to finding true *joy*.

~

God is the happiest being in the universe. We will have joy to the degree we live like Him.

~

Dad had an epiphany on discerning the difference between joy vs. pleasure while teaching at the MTC. He was concurrently teaching the 17-year-old Sunday School class in Alpine, Utah, and so had a unique opportunity to compare and contrast the youth right before going on a mission as opposed to the attitude of those studying at the MTC. The students in the ward were wealthy and had access to nearly every form of entertainment and pleasure they could desire. Meanwhile, the young missionaries at the MTC (about the same age) were confined to a building with cinder block styled walls without windows—the architecture and design closer to a prison than a home. They studied from early morning to evening, only taking breaks for meals or short sporting recreation. They had three teachers, three hours each, and no diversion.

---

4 Joseph Smith, letter to Nancy Rigdon, circa Mid-April 1842, The Joseph Smith Papers; emphasis added.

However, the students in the MTC acted as though they were happier and experiencing more peace than the kids in Alpine. The missionaries were discovering a love for the Gospel, writing letters of apology to their parents and others they may have wronged—truly experiencing a change of heart. Dad started surveying these young missionaries, individually and in group settings: "When were you happier? Before coming to the MTC or now?" Dad said he never had one student admit they were happier before, and their conduct certainly added a second witness to their comments!

The wheels began turning in Dad's head—there was something to learn here. With Utah among the leading states in the nation for depression,[5] Dad always observed and commented to us: "Are we losing the search for happiness because we are focused on ourselves—only to discover that this journey ends in a dead end road of empty loneliness?"

OVERCOMING LOW SELF ESTEEM BY EMBRACING JOY, NOT PLEASURE

Hannah remembers: I was around 15 or 16 when Dad watched a film with us titled *Bless You, Prison*. It is the story of a Romanian Christian woman who was imprisoned by the Communists. She endured solitary confinement, isolation, hard labor, beatings and so forth. Through her experience, she drew closer to God and the film depicts her journey, while also portraying some of her suffering. I remember watching the film and wondering, *"I think she is happier than I am. She seems more at peace, more full of joy and has more purpose than I do. But I live in heaven compared to her hell. How can this be?"* Shortly after, we watched *God's Outlaw: The Story of William Tyndale*. Again, this theme impressed me. How could they be so happy? They had more joy than I did, and they had

---

5   Ken Alltucker, "Depression, suicide rates highest in Mountain West states," *USA Today*, December 6, 2018, https://www.usatoday.com/in-depth/news/health/2018/12/06/depression-rates-rise-utah-looking-slow-increase/2213071002/.

nothing!! I also watched my Dad and noticed how happy he was—without a lot of pleasure in his life. He loved the scriptures more than anything, and he had a sense of peace and inner confidence.

I decided to experiment on this strange phenomenon. I started reading my scriptures more, I prayed harder, I tried to be more obedient, and I made sacrifices—I wanted the peace they had. I wanted that connection with God. Slowly, over time, clarity came as I tasted *real joy*, and its counterfeit—pleasure—began losing its charm. Sure, there was a rush of excitement, or a trigger of dopamine when I chased after pleasure with food, fun activities, or movies—and it lasted for a few hours, maybe even days, but then it was gone. If I was honest with myself, the whole time I was still empty. I was having fun, but deep down, I was unhappy. I compared myself with the other teens around me; I was conscious about my appearance, and I wanted to fit in. I worried whether guys would like me the way they liked other girls in our circle. I wanted to be smart so I would be respected—but then I was frustrated when I didn't measure up. I would spend hours writing my stories or reading a novel and then discover I was irritable and didn't feel I had real worth.

Curiously, the more I gave up what I wanted to serve my family, to learn and model God's nature, and the harder I worked on our family projects, the more I began to experience a deep, powerful sense of pure joy, peace, contentment, and confidence in levels I had never known before. I felt happy and fulfilled climbing into bed exhausted after working in the office all day with my family, or turning into a red lobster from a sunburn while sweating down on our homestead, after hours moving and bedding pipe in the rocky soil. Knowing I had made someone's life better and knowing God was pleased with me filled my soul with a joy and peace that is indescribable and unattainable any other way.

My Dad gave me the opportunity to learn this lesson by (1) teaching the Gospel principle of joy vs. pleasure, (2) structuring our life and school schedules around hard work and service-based projects, and (3) modeling true joy in his own life so we naturally sought after the same happiness he had. Soon the difference between pleasure and joy became so contrasted that I naturally clung to the lasting, substantive joy. My old life just wasn't worth it! I had found the tree of life, and its fruit filled me with the happiness and belonging I had always desired!

"By Their Fruits"

Every endowed member of the Church covenants with God to give their time, talents, and everything with which the Lord has blessed them to build the Kingdom of God on earth. Dad took his pledge literally, and he taught us that true joy and inner confidence could only be found by yielding your life to God. We had to lose our life . . . to save it.

Cynics have often grumbled and complained that Dad was extreme and radical. Our response is a simple question: what is the fruit? "Ye shall know them by their fruits," the Son of God taught His disciples. The fruit born through Dad's personal interactions, his legacy with the Joseph Smith Foundation, and the results from his children who followed his example speak for themselves. We can bear our certain testimony that joy—real lasting joy—conversion, family unity and miracles only come from living the Lord's way.

CHAPTER
Seven

"TO KNOW THE THINGS MY FATHER HAD SEEN"

". . . I had desired to know the things that my father had seen, and believing that the Lord was able to make them known unto me . . . "

— 1 Nephi 11:1

This chapter is written by Hannah regarding her experience gaining a testimony and witness for herself.

Critics have accused James Stoddard of brainwashing his kids to get them to adopt such a 'crazy' lifestyle of consecration, service, and passion for defending the Restoration. Only a cult could convince someone to lay down their life for Christ, right? Everyone will judge our family as they choose; however, I want to share why I am here. I want to share my testimony of how God changed my heart and mercifully condescended to give me a sure witness of the "things my father had seen." I am here, not because of my Dad, but because of my own personal experience with God.

I never really doubted the existence of God but always wanted to know more—I wanted to know why the Gospel 'worked.' I can remember being seven years old and praying, "God, if you are real, *prove* it to me. If I turn on the light switch in the garage and it doesn't go on, that will be a miracle, and I will know You are real." I flipped the switch, and immediately the light bulb burst into light just like any other boring day. Hmmm. I flipped the light back off and went into the house. Suddenly I stopped. The light switch test was silly. I knew God was real—it wasn't even a question. I remember writing in my journal: "I turned on the light and it still turned on but I still believe in God."

I've always been one who likes to have a plan and execute it exactly. When I was young, I prided myself on being 'good.' And 'good' meant I followed the program. The *Friend* magazine talked about kids reading the Book of Mormon before they were baptized, so I buckled down and read through it before I turned eight. In Primary they asked us to memorize the Articles of Faith. Check! Faith in God Award? Check. Personal Progress Awards? Check. Every seminary assignment? Double check. I tried to follow rules and felt pretty satisfied with myself. I enjoyed studying the Gospel and read every *Ensign* magazine cover to cover. I started reading *Doctrines of Salvation* and *Answers to Gospel Questions* when I was 10. Inherently, I felt an interest in the Gospel and a love for God. I wanted to 'be good.' But I wasn't the person God wanted me to become—I had more potential and I had a *lot* of pride to overcome.

There was one fundamental missing link: I had not surrendered my life to God. Being good was more about *myself* and how I saw my identity than about submission. This lack of a change of heart was evident in my relationships with my siblings and how I chose to spend my free time. By the world's standards, I was an exemplary child. But by God's standards, I fell very short.

Experiencing Love Beyond Comprehension

When I was 13 years old, Mom decided she wanted to build a house up the street from where we were renting in Saratoga Springs. Dad was working full time as a software engineer, his health wasn't the best, and he was not convinced building a home at this time was the wisest plan. However, the project was important to my Mom and so managing the home, maintaining the homeschool, caring for the little ones (including Mary, who was only a few months old), preparing meals, and so forth fell on my shoulders.

Thankfully, Dad had always encouraged us to learn home skills. I was cooking most of the meals from scratch when I was 11! But taking over the home was a new adventure, and it pushed me to my very limit. As weeks turned into months, my patience and energy began running extremely thin. I was exhausted. One cold night, after a long hard day and a late dinner. I was near the point of tears and just kept telling myself to go a little longer before I could crash. When I was finally able to drag myself upstairs to my room, I shut the door behind me and just cried in the darkness. I cried and cried as if my heart would break, releasing the stress of the last few months. I didn't know how I could keep going. Slowly, I looked up. The view out my window had a stunning panorama of Utah Lake. It was dark and a reflection of the lights on the opposite side from Orem and Provo twinkled and sparkled over the water.

Unexpectedly, the most powerful feeling of love and comfort washed over me, encircling me with the most profound compassion, nobility, and affection I had ever felt in my life. I knew without the smallest shadow of doubt that God was not only real, but that He knew exactly who I was and *loved* me with such a strong, deep, unwavering love that I could never have imagined existed. I felt power—but it wasn't controlling, it wasn't overpowering, it wasn't an 'earthquake'—it was strong, noble, pure, and selfless. I walked out of that room a changed person, and that caused me to fall on my knees and tell God that I would give my life to Him. Anyone who lived by and expressed that kind of pure, selfless love, I wanted to become like. How could I not want to love and obey someone who felt that kind of noble compassion for me? Now I understood why my Dad loved God so much. Now I understood why he would feast on the scriptures, preferring them to any other book. The spirit of God was a priceless treasure.

I started studying everything I could, not because I was smart or important, but because I wanted to know more. I wanted to learn how to become a real Christian! God began showing me my flaws, and in many ways, began breaking my heart—tearing down my walls of self-importance bit by bit. I saw where I had been selfish and prideful. God convicted me in how I treated my little brothers and sisters. He challenged me to be more respectful to Dad and Mom, even in moments of conflict. I began recognizing my slothfulness, and my weaknesses seemed to stand out more boldly than ever. I also began to recognize that no one could release me from those weaknesses but God. Some days, I recognized something I was doing wrong, but to be honest, I didn't really *want* to change. I didn't feel Godly sorrow, and so I prayed and prayed for God to soften my heart so that I could feel new remorse for my sins. Slowly, piece by piece, day by day, sacrifice by sacrifice, He changed my heart.

Gaining My Own Witness

As I began to understand the Gospel in a new way, and as I began to see and experience the joy that is found in following in the footsteps of Jesus Christ, I also became aware of mocking voices. Many people thought my Dad was crazy. Did he really think he was going to start a foundation with a bunch of kids? Was it really worth these sacrifices? Wasn't he taking the Gospel to an extreme? And what about his kids? Some told Dad we were going to become rebellious and uneducated from this lifestyle.

I had always been a stubborn and determined person. I did what I thought was right, no matter who thought otherwise, so as I listened to both sides of this argument between my Dad's vision and others who were skeptical, I started thinking. At the end of the day, this was *my* life. I was the one who would live with the consequences forever. I wanted to know: was my Dad a visionary dreamer, chasing an empty life philosophy? Maybe the critics were right, and this would all end in ruin and disaster. I had to stand on my own two feet and decide for *myself* what was true. I wasn't going to rely on Dad, Mom, or anyone else!

Around the time I was 15 years old, I decided it was high time to receive a solid witness for myself.

For a period of time, I did a lot of thinking and praying. I asked God to show me if my Dad really was being inspired. I wanted to know God's design for families and what He expected of me. I trusted my Savior. I believed He would stand behind what was best, but I wanted to *know*. Like Nephi of old, I too had a mother who sometimes wavered, I had some siblings who were on board, and other siblings who struggled. So I cried to the Lord for wisdom and insight—and just as the Lord had answered this mighty prophet of old, the Lord answered *me*. I came to know for myself what God had asked our family to do, and His will and path to obtain it. I knew that our projects weren't about us, they weren't about Dad, and they weren't about any of our supporters—they were for the Lord. That was a pivotal year in my life, and I remember it as one of the best. I had never been so excited for the future! It was as if a new world had opened up before me.

Dad had already produced one documentary and started a few websites, and I dived in, fully committed now. This wasn't Dad's project, this was *my* project. I helped him write a letter to a well-known Evangelical Christian demonstrating that the Book of Mormon was a second witness of Jesus Christ and the Bible.[1] I started learning Adobe Photoshop, and we began turning Dad's notes for the Book of Mormon parallels into an actual timeline. We spent *hours* in that office creating the For Our Day model that we now offer as a poster. Only the Lord knows the days and weeks of patient research and graphic design it took to make that project a reality, but I learned more about the Book of Mormon from that work alone than in all my previous study. I also started my own girls discussion group called "Maidens with a Mission" to ignite the fire of faith in others.

---

1   "A Letter to My Christian Friends," Joseph Smith Foundation, https://josephsmithfoundation.org/a-letter-to-my-christian-friends/.

Surrendering My Life to Christ

In 2012, we started working on the documentary that would become *For Our Day: Covenant on the Land*. We had a video studio in our home, but there was a lot of trial and error filming interviews and editing. Our goal was to release it at Rod Meldrum's Book of Mormon Evidence Expo in April 2013. Looking back, I honestly have *no idea* how we finished it . . . and we almost didn't.

At this point, I had my own witness that our family was supposed to undertake these projects, but I also had a lot of my own goals as well. I wanted to write novels, I wanted to build a company for young women, and many times I got distracted on the Internet following different conservative groups and movements. I wanted to do everything, and while there was nothing I was doing that anyone would think of as *bad*, the simple fact of the matter is that there are only 24 hours in each day, and God has a plan for those 24 hours. Filling in bonus activities of our own choice is nice . . . but some things get left out. And for me, too often God's higher priority moved to second place, while I pursued everything *I* wanted to do. There was time for both, right?

Reality struck one winter night as the deadline for finishing *Covenant on the Land* loomed closer. How had the deadline crept up on us so quickly? We weren't ready. Dad said we could only do what we could do, and we just had to be content with that, but as I lay in my bed quietly thinking, a deep sense of conviction weighed heavily on me. I wanted to pray and say, "God will provide, and we trust Him," but I knew I hadn't done my part. If I was honest, deep inside I knew I hadn't given it my all and now, when I needed His comfort and assurance of my standing with Him, it wasn't there. The sense of the consequences began to be impressed on my mind with ever-increasing intensity. I knew what God wanted, and this was real life. This wasn't a video game where I could just hit reset. This documentary wasn't going to magically get done. Then, this greater question came to me: how would I answer to God when I got to the other side?

Finally, in turmoil I was driven to my knees, and I prayed hard—harder than I had ever prayed to that point in my life. I begged God for forgiveness, and I pleaded for mercy, despite my weaknesses. I pledged that from that point forward I would surrender my life to Him. I would truly be a Christian—I would take His name upon me. "Hannah Stoddard's" life was over. I would now bear the name of Jesus Christ. I humbly petitioned the Lord to help us finish this video, and promised Him that if He did, I would faithfully follow Him to the end. Peace came over me and after a time, I crawled back into bed and fell asleep.

Miracles occurred, and *For Our Day: Covenant on the Land* was released in April 2013, on time and on schedule. We announced it at the Book of Mormon Evidence Expo in Sandy, Utah, and then went to work on a sequel, *For Our Day: Divinely Sanctioned Governments*. This time, I was committed to give it my all. I wasn't going to make any of my former slothful mistakes!

Progress moved steadily along as spring turned into summer. We had a family garden we worked in every morning before returning to the house to work inside. One morning I was pulling weeds when I felt a distinct impression. I felt that the Lord was pleased with the direction I had taken in my life and that He loved me. There was that noble, pure love again. In return for my sacrifices I felt a promise that no matter what happened, this next documentary would be finished on time. I was grateful for the experience but didn't think much of it. We were on schedule and everything was going well.

However, as the summer progressed and our fall deadline loomed closer, everything seemed to go wrong. Computer equipment failed, there was family friction, interruptions from outside commitments, and strange video issues that we couldn't sort out—and it all seemed to appear out of nowhere. One evening when we were all together in the office, our exhaustion drove us to the point of tears. Dad gave up. He said, "It's not going to get done. No reason to kill ourselves. Let's just face the truth and accept that we're not going to get it done." He walked out of the office with my brother and sister.

I sat alone, stunned and heartbroken—but what could be done? Suddenly, to my mind came the promise the Lord had made to me months earlier. I felt certain it was still in effect and new determination surged within me. I spent a few minutes doing some quick figuring before I marched out of that office and faced my family in the dining room, stubbornly committed and ready to debate. "Guys, we CAN'T give up now! We are so close! I think we can finish it."

My Dad looked at me in disbelief. "You do??"

"Sure we can!" I said confidently—but honestly, I was still trying to convince myself. I laid out a few ideas, and after dinner we returned to our war room (aka office) and went back to work. I still don't know how it happened . . . but that DVD was finished as well! A bit rough in a few places and a few sections had some rushed sound effects that we corrected on a second run, but it was *finished*! I never forgot that experience—when you give your all, the Lord gives His, and miracles result.

I would need that lesson many times in the future. On several other DVDs, our roles reversed and my Dad was the one trying to convince *me* that the impossible was possible. I remember one night crying in my bedroom while we were in the middle of *Unlocking the Mystery of the Two Prophets*. It was one of the hardest periods of my life, with so many different factors and situations weighing me down. My Dad came in and sat down on my bed. He simply said, "Hannah, you have to *believe*. God can do all things, but you have to believe He can." I told him I knew God could do anything, but my Dad said, "Well, if you *truly* believe, your actions will reflect that." I spent a lot of time pondering after that conversation, often while taking a morning run. "*Do I really believe?*"

Sacrifice Brings Forth Blessings

One of the greatest motivators for me personally was watching the blessings that came after we finished each project. Since beginning in 2008, emails and phone calls have consistently come from grateful individuals sharing how a documentary or book changed their life. I have learned that sacrifice truly does bring forth the blessings of heaven. For example, in 2014 and early 2015, I was offered the opportunity to join a group of women at the United Nations headquarters in New York to speak in defense

Sledding with the kids

of the family. I was ecstatic! I had always known supporting family roles was part of my mission, and this would be an incredible experience. However, we were in the middle of producing *The Prophet Joseph: More Than We Know*, and as I prepared to fill out the paperwork for the trip back East, I stopped—realizing that there was no way I would be able to accomplish *both* of these projects. I would have to cancel one. I called my Dad at work for his advice. He was quiet, but then said, "I don't know what the right thing is, Peps. You just decide whatever you think is best and the right thing to do. We can put off the video. That is fine. You just decide what the Lord wants right now."

Great . . . having the weight of this choice resting on me was sobering. I took some time to think about it. We had already produced four documentaries; surely delaying one for a few months wouldn't be that big of a deal. But when I prayed, I couldn't deny that deep in my heart I knew the Lord wanted me to make a sacrifice. *"But Lord,"* I protested, *"I could do so much good! They will be doing news interviews and short videos. I may get a chance to speak; we will have a blog, etc.*" Sitting at home in an office editing video in order to release a documentary, with no way of knowing how many would actually see or be impacted by it, didn't seem so glamorous. In the end, I made the decision to trust the answer to my prayer—I canceled my place on the trip so I could finish the documentary. After completing the last edit and sending it off to the replicators, I hoped my choice would prove to have been worth it.

The Lord works through small and simple things. As time passed—after the trial of my faith—I was overwhelmed to see that the Lord's way is *always* best. Looking back, I realized that this documentary needed to be finished right then. An unforeseen move later that year could have delayed its production for two years! In addition to many emails and positive responses on this project, several families returned to the Church because of the impact of this film on their lives. They explained to me personally how the timing of its release was critical and clearly orchestrated by God. One of my closest team members in the Joseph Smith Foundation gained a testimony of certain doctrines while watching it, which resulted in her assisting with successive projects that have changed *thousands* of lives. When I think of how close I was to delaying God's will, I am eternally grateful that I set aside what I thought was best—what I wanted to do—and instead chose the Lord's path.

Growing up with my Dad and the Joseph Smith Foundation has taught me that the Lord doesn't need wealth, talent, or position to do His work. He is searching for those willing to give Him their heart. He has all power, and He can do *anything*. He stands at the door and knocks—hoping each of us will accept His invitation, allow Him to work in our life, and accomplish miracles we never dreamed were possible. Will we open the door?

CHAPTER
Eight

IT'S ABOUT JOY!

". . . [M]en are, that they might have joy."

— 2 Nephi 2:25

Life was not all work—far from it. The same creativity Dad poured into the videos, he also poured into activities and recreation—and oh how he loved buying toys for his kids! It was almost an obsession. At one point, we even had two sets of playground equipment *inside* our house so the kids had a place to play during the winter. Eliza (5 years old at the time) said she liked dollhouses, and before we knew it . . . two large dollhouses arrived at our home. We have boxes and boxes of toys stored on our homestead property because we can never fit them in one house at the same time: blocks, Lincoln Logs, lots of Legos, different magnet games, outdoor basketball hoops, indoor basketball hoops, a kids bowling set, historical dress-ups, art kits, puppets—the list could go on and on!

PLAYING WITH DAD

Leah remembers: My Dad loved playing with us (Lego castles! Box forts! Wiffleball! You name it!). He really enjoyed playing with kids. A few months before he passed away, we were playing a game where we'd throw a ball

back and forth in a group. You had to be ready, because you never knew if the person with the ball was going to throw it to you or someone else. He had to do it sitting down, because he was too weak to stand.

If Dad could've done anything, and there were no starving children in India, or a world falling apart, I think he would:

Sit back and play with his kids

Grow plants

Make videos

Write songs

Relax, and . . .

. . . hopefully, he'd be able to catch up on sleeping

Making faces in watermelon slices with Dad

Dad showed by example that living a Christian life did *not* mean eliminating joy, activities, and relaxation. Instead, he simply applied some simple principles when choosing what recreations would or would not be part of our family:

- Does this activity have an intentional *purpose*?

- Does this activity encourage our bond as a family? Or does it alienate us from one another?

- Does this activity allow us to develop hands on skills or strengthen our mind? Or is it a waste of valuable time?

- Does this activity cultivate Godlike attributes such as nobility, kindness, refinement, honor, integrity, or humility? Or does it foster silliness, light-mindedness, pride, addiction, and possibly even negative emotions such as anxiety or aggression?

- Does this activity allow us to better serve others?

• Does this activity bring the Spirit of God into our home? Or does it drive it away?

President Joseph F. Smith, the son of Hyrum Smith and the sixth President of the Church, counseled:

 We should train ourselves to find pleasure in that which invigorates, not stupefies and destroys the body; that which leads upward and not down; that which brightens, not dulls and stunts the intellect; that which elevates and exalts the spirit, not that clogs and depresses it. So shall we please the Lord, enhance our own enjoyment, and save ourselves and our children from impending sins . . .[1]

For this reason, our family chose to focus on games and activities that drew us closer to God and aligned with counsel from inspired leaders. Early Presidents of the Church had taught the Saints against playing any game with the element of chance, so these were eliminated in our home.[2] We didn't play video

---

1   Joseph F. Smith, "The Evil of Cards," *Improvement Era*, June 1911, no. 8, 738.

2   The First Presidency stated: ". . . we say again to the people that no kind of chance game, guessing contest, or raffling device can be approved in any entertainment under the auspices of our Church organizations.

The desire to get something of value for little or nothing is pernicious . . . In reply to a question as to whether raffling and games of chance are justifiable when the purposes to be accomplished are good, this was said: 'We say emphatically, No. Raffle is only a modified name of gamble.'" Joseph F. Smith, *Improvement Era*, vol. 12, December 1908, 143-144.

Joseph Fielding Smith also said, "Nothing good comes out of card games or games of chance. There are numerous ways in which we may obtain wholesome amusement and recreation which is beneficial to both body and mind. In games where cards are used usually 'stakes' are played for, and betting is done. Someone will obtain the 'stakes,' but no one really wins, for the one who obtains the 'stakes' has lost part of his manhood which is difficult to regain. There seems to be an urge in human nature which leads many men and women to seek to obtain something for nothing . . . There is a lure in all games of chance which Satan places before them, and in their greed or selfish desire for gain they take the

Making cookies with Dad

games. We didn't watch movies that glorified magic, witches, violence, immorality, selfishness, or dysfunctional family life.[3] Per President Harold B. Lee and Ezra Taft Benson's counsel, we did not listen to music with a rock beat.[4] We simply tried to follow the 13th Article of Faith: "If there is anything virtuous, lovely, or of good report or praiseworthy, we seek after these things."

The best leisure and recreation is productive, refined, and brings the family closer to God.

---

uncertain bait far less innocently than does a fish which grabs the angler's hook." Joseph Fielding Smith, *Answers to Gospel Questions*, vol. 1 (Salt Lake City: Deseret Book Company, 1957), 92.

3   See Chapter 12, "Our Philosophy on Movies."

4   See Chapter 11, "Music: The Forgotten Language of the Heart."

President Joseph F. Smith taught, "One's character may be determined in some measure by the quality of one's amusements." And "Tell me what amusements you like best and whether your amusements have become a ruling passion in your life, and I will tell you what you are."[5] Dad took this to heart, and we only participated in activities after thoughtful and intentional consideration of whether they would uphold or detract from developing Christlike attributes. In addition to an abundance of useful and educational toys, these were some of our favorite recreational activities as a family:

Cooking: The Word of Wisdom instructs the Latter-day Saint to focus on a diet with vegetables, fruits, seeds, grains, herbs, and so forth—harvested in their natural season. Dad always maintained that God clearly intended for food to taste good—so if it wasn't palatable, we were doing something wrong! We experimented in the kitchen with different spices, muti-cultural dishes, and we even bought a Mongolian grill for cooking!

---

5 Joseph F. Smith, "The Social Effects of Card Playing," in *Juvenile Instructor*, Vol. 38, September 1, 1903, 528-529.

When we lived in Colorado, we sometimes heard of large food giveaways from local grocery stores who were unable to sell produce that was getting old. Once there was a large shipment of bananas, and we packed our car to the roof. At home, we peeled and froze those bananas in big freezer bags, and for the next year or so, we used them in smoothies and Dad's famous "eggnog drink." He would blend the bananas with frozen milk cubes, nutmeg, and cinnamon. Another time, there was a strawberry giveaway, and we blended these with lime juice

We caught someone in the cookies!

to create a kosher 'Strawberry-Lime Rickey.' Oh, they were so good! "You can have as much as you want!" Dad would say. We filled and refilled our cups until we thought we would burst. Those were the days!

A year or two before he passed away, the kids wanted to make cookies, leading Dad to creatively invent 'Hebrew cookies.' We were reading a book on ancient Hebrew characters,[6] so he led us in shaping the cookie dough into ancient Hebrew characters to create different words: 'Joseph,' 'Jesus,' 'Ephraim,' etc. Dad knew that applying learning with hands-on activities was not only fun and memorable, but it would improve our retention of the knowledge we were acquiring.

Singing & Music: There are few things that bring the Spirit of God into a home with greater power and effectiveness than

---

6 Frank T. Seekins, *Hebrew Word Pictures* (Phoenix: Living Word Pictures Inc., 1994).

Singing around our Hanukkah candles. We've celebrated a Latter-day Saint version of Hanukkah for a number of years due to Jewish ancestry and symbolic parallels with the Gospel.

music. Singing together as a family creates bonds, strengthens unity, and teaches the Gospel to children far more effectively than most sermons. Dad always emphasized this in our home, and in December, we had a list of Christmas carols we would sing. We often sang on the way home from working on our farm, which was about an hour away from our home. Dad would say, "Start us out on a song, Peps [Hannah's nickname]!" and we would sing and sing until our spirits were cheered up. Dad even wrote two Christmas carols, both inspired by the Book of Mormon. We would search through old folk songs, find our favorite tunes, and copy the lyrics into our family songbook—or rewrite them if we thought they should be improved. Dad bought penny whistles for all the kids and harmonicas for some of the boys. He asked us to learn these unique instruments to add variety in our own family ensemble. When Eliza was five or six, she would walk around the house blowing her whistle until we thought our eardrums would explode. One day, we were quietly studying when suddenly the silence was shattered by Eliza playing her recorder in the office. Eliza had found a computer and discovered how to Google "recorder lessons" on YouTube. The music was far from melodious but Dad loved to hear her play. We never did finish learning how to play those whistles, but it is certainly on our list now as we work to continue our family legacy! Our work is not over—it is really just beginning!

Sports: We have numerous memories of Dad joining us in going to the park with family friends and playing Wiffle ball, tag, soccer, running in the sprinklers, and basketball. We had a running joke that teams were always divided between the 'thinkers' versus the 'dreamers.' The 'thinkers' would advocate their superiority, because Dad was constantly emphasizing critical thinking. But the 'dreamers' argued that "it's the dream that counts." Since the authors of this book are divided, this text will remain neutral and allow the reader to decide which team name truly is best.

And then the wrestling and boxing matches . . . impossible to describe in words. Yes, the girls definitely participated! We had bikes, scooters, trikes, and big wheels—unfortunately, none with motors, because Dad said we needed exercise. (Sigh.)

Dad would allow us to use old shed pieces and lumber from nearby dumpsters to build our own play 'city.' Some of our best memories!

It was an enjoyable way to get exercise, fresh air, natural sunlight, and have fun together. Dad would take children for one-on-one walks to talk while the rest of us raced on ahead. When Hannah and Leah were around ten and eight respectively, they can remember peddling those scooters around and around the park while they had a story contest—each of them entertaining the other with the latest 'novel' they were writing.

Active Games: Among many other active games, Dad invented something called 'Scripture Charades.' We would divide into teams and decide on a scene from a scripture story: Mormon burying the plates, Captain Moroni with the Title of Liberty, Nephi building the boat, Daniel in the lion's den, or many of the parables from the New Testament. Without making a verbal sound or utilizing props, we had to act out the scene, and the audience had to guess which scripture we were representing. Common storylines were easy, but it got pretty complicated when someone would choose an unheard of allegory from Ezekiel, or perhaps an obscure reference from the Old Testament. It was a humorous way to stretch our knowledge of the scriptures and test our accuracy in acting it out.

Reading Together: Many nights we tried to shut down at a reasonable time and curl up while someone read a book aloud: *In Freedom's Cause, Sense and Sensibility, Emma, North and South* . . . education didn't end when the sun went down, and Dad had a healthy appreciation for classical literature. On other nights, music played quietly while we read our scriptures or wrote in our journals. It gave us time to refocus, evaluate our day, and prepare for another adventure in the morning.

LITERATURE—HANNAH REMEMBERS:

Some of my best memories involve discussing literature with my Dad. He had such a good balance of being masculine, tough, familiar with tools, skilled at sports—and at the same time, he felt and expressed emotion so deeply, he loved to dance, he wrote poetry, and he was appreciative of literature. He could get a little overly defensive of Jane Austen though . . . she was *not* to be questioned! He always said, "*Real* men appreciate Jane Austen and clean classic literature." I can remember listening to *Emma* in the car with him, and he would laugh at the humor and just smile during lines with clever wit. His favorite novel was *Mansfield Park*, he said, because the theme spoke of being true to your principles. He loved *Persuasion* as well because of the "deep emotion and feeling." He attempted to cultivate a love for the arts in all of us!

Movies: As we grew up, we would often gather as a family to watch films. This wasn't just an occasional activity, but a central part of our recreation. We watched hundreds of motion pictures and documentaries on Christian persecution,[7] Communism,[8] the Holocaust, abortion,[9] natural and conventional medicine, the Hungarian Revolution, education, the Constitution—and the list goes on! These were films that taught the good and exposed the bad—the light contrasted against the darkness in this world.

Dad always remarked how film could teach more in one hour than books could in 10. Why is this? Because the combination of stunning visuals, music, voice, color, and animation create a crude, man-made version of a 'vision' experience, if you will. Dad would often point out how the aesthetics, camera angles, lighting, etc., of a movie contributed to the spirit behind the film. This powerful tool could and is being used for good and evil. Choose to use it for good! Some of our most impactful and effective family councils and discussions occurred surrounding a film. Don't underestimate its power!

Rather than mindless entertainment, our family movie time was highly educational and instructive. We *never* watched a movie without Dad pausing it at least two or three times (if not more) to stop and teach. "Why did Elizabeth Bennett connect love and respect in *Pride and Prejudice*? Why did Stonewall Jackson in *Gods & Generals* say he wasn't afraid when the bullets were flying around him? Why is this scene in *Beauty and the Beast* denigrating mothers? Why is Edith the heroine in *The Inheritance*? How is Eric Liddell a perfect example of *living* Christian faith in *On Wings of Eagles*, instead of falling into the trap of preachy sermonizing? How is our family trying to be like William Tyndale in *God's Outlaw*? Why did Dmitri succumb to pressure in the Russian prison, but then later have the courage to stand firm in *The Printing*?"

---

7 *China Cry* (1990), *For Greater Glory* (2012), *On Wings of Eagles* (2016), *Free Burma Rangers* (2020), *The Insanity of God* (2016), *The Least of These* (2019), *Bless You, Prison* (2002), *Flame in the Wind* (1971), *God's Outlaw* (1986)

8 *Messenger of the Truth* (2013), *Night Crossing* (1982), *The Printing* (1990), *Tortured for Christ* (2018), *Sabina: Tortured for Christ - The Nazi Years* (2022), *Karol: The Man Who Became Pope* (2005)

9 *Gosnell* (2008), *Unplanned* (2019)

HOW FAMILY MOVIES HELP YOU THROUGH DIFFICULT LIFE EXPERIENCES

Mary remembers: I am very thankful that my Dad always provided us with good movies. They have taught me so many good things. I am very surprised at the many times when I think of something that I saw in a movie and it will help me make better decisions, guide me through a hard trial, or just help me to be better. Just recently, I was really struggling. There were some really crazy things going on, and I was really worried about what was going to happen to me. Just then, I remembered a scene from the *Torchlighters: The Story of Corrie Ten Boom* movie where Corrie and Betsy are in a concentration camp, and it is really hard, and Betsy (Corrie's sister) tells Corrie not to worry and that God has a plan. Thinking about their example really helped me to understand that God has a reason for everything and that we just need to trust Him.

Another thing that really helped me in this movie was the part where Betsy tells Corrie that she felt very sorry for the officers at that camp after one of the officers had just beat her, because she knew Hitler would fall, and then the soldiers would be alone and really confused, while she and Corrie would always have God. I really marveled at how she was so quick to forgive them even though they had done so many wrong things to them and that she even felt sorry for them. This example, in addition to my sister Hannah's words, helped me to try and forgive my Mom.[10] I know I wouldn't be in the same place today if I wouldn't have watched all of those good movies. Watching good movies can positively impact your life in more ways than you can imagine—you just have to give it a chance.

---

10   See Chapter 15, "Healing & Beauty from Ashes."

WATCHING 400 MOVIES

Julie, a friend, remembers: After being crushed as a mother, and finally resurfacing after having one child leave the Church—and another attempt to take his life, I realized just how much my home had been compromised by the current culture, and what role that culture had played in the breakdown of my family. This is when I humbly asked God: "How do I begin to take my family out of the murkiness of this world?"

The answer to the question I asked came with an assignment through James Stoddard. He knew of my desire and struggles and suggested that if I was really wanting to remove the worldly influences and restore my home— aligned with scripture, then I needed to re-educate my family from the philosophies of this world.

How would this be done? How does one re-educate their partially-grown family? What does that look like, and how long would it take? James told me about ZionTube[11] and its purpose and that there were over 400 movies on it to watch. He said: "watch a movie and find a principle in it to defend, and then write up a review with your kids and submit it under the movie when finished."

400 MOVIES? WAS HE CRAZY?? I had just started eliminating movies in my home and was enjoying the peace from the entertainment world, so there was no way I wanted to now go watch that many movies. However, I did feel this was inspired as he spoke about how "movies had the power to change lives faster than a book." He also explained how these movies were all 'screened' with correct principles in them and would help my family see, and *feel* quicker than anything I could ever say in hopes to reach my children.

---

11 Learn more about ZionTube and find hundreds of free movies at https://josephsmithfoundation.org/ziontube.

So, for our homeschooling, we began 're-educating' using the movies suggested on ZionTube. Each weekend we would take a movie, watch it, and pause to discuss what we were learning. All of a sudden, we went from the traditional weekend entertainment—to even using a video daily to gradually correct patterns of indoctrination that we had absorbed.

I was seeing instant results in my family— from lively dinner discussions about the latest film and how we were changed by it—to learning how to write and speak what we were feeling through our movie reviews. This 're-education' program transformed our home and woke us up to the hidden agendas that had lulled us to sleep through the name of 'entertainment.' I will always be grateful to James for this *inspired* movie assignment and how it helped rescue three of my children and is now reaching my grandchildren!

Around 2001-2003, Dad started a simple, basic website at StoddardHome.org (currently nonexistent) where he posted a list of movies and why the film was recommended. He had spent hundreds of hours sorting through video stores, bookstores, websites, and so forth, and he wanted to save other families from 'reinventing the wheel.' This simple movie table later became 'ZionTube,' a searchable compilation of movies and documentaries that now resides on the Joseph Smith Foundation website, blessing the lives of hundreds—even thousands—of families. Dad was always thinking outside his home, always innovating to serve and help others. He never kept knowledge to himself—he just wanted to lift and build.

Social Activities: Many times—when working at our homestead property—friends would visit to help weed and water. When it was lunchtime, we all retired to our eating area for "Happy Hour," as little Mary called it. 'Happy Hour' was just that—a time to laugh, crack jokes, and talk about . . . just about every subject on the planet! It was the highlight of our work day.

Other more formal activities with friends often featured family dancing (English country dance, square dance, the Virginia Reel, etc.) and sword fighting. Dad taught us how to waltz right in our living room! In a world where so many social activities encourage children to divide into groups, segregate the popular from the unpopular, and discourage siblings from having common friends—our activities were aimed to bring everyone together.

United . . . Not Divided

Through experience, trial, error, and success, we have learned that (a) activities don't have to be silly or wasteful to be fun, (b) how to recognize the difference between activities that contribute and those that detract, and finally, (c) that choosing purposeful leisure is rejuvenating and brings one closer to God. Instead of encouraging us to selfishly invest in ourselves, we invested in activities that brought a spirit of refinement, charity, unity, and strengthened bonds between us as a family and as siblings. We learned how to use relaxation and recreation to expand and grow Godlike characteristics. God is the perfect scientist, the perfect artist, the perfect sportsman, the perfect chef, the perfect designer, the perfect gardener, and the perfect humorist. If we want to have joy, we have to become like Him in every area! Pursuing that goal has left us with so many memories of laughter, peace, happiness, and joy, when we remember growing up as a 'Stoddard.'

CHAPTER
Nine

HIGHLAND CATHEDRAL

WHERE COUNTRY LIFE IS REAL LIVING

*"And it came to pass that I, Nephi, did cause my people to
be industrious, and to labor with their hands."*

— 2 Nephi 5:17

In 2013, shortly after finishing *For Our Day: Covenant on
the Land*, Dad made a surprising announcement. While we
always had a garden and worked with him outside, he felt
it was time to take outdoor labor to an entirely new level. Our
family was going to buy land in Sanpete County and start our
own homestead.

Dad understood the essential nature of manual labor in the
development of children. Learning to work hard in the sun,
embrace sweat, and use tools would not only build character,
but provide knowledge for navigating the 'last days.' Dad didn't
want his kids to be limited to technology and office work. He
wanted them to have the freedom and health that comes with
provident living and working directly in the soil.

The hunt for a piece of property began with hours and days
spent driving through the Sanpete Valley. Our brother Joseph
was buried in Manti, and we looked at lots there, but soon felt
drawn to the east side of the valley. As a family, we narrowed

possible options down to two pieces of land. The first was a beautiful property with a stream, trees, and good soil in Mt. Pleasant. The other was barren and dry—with rocks and sagebrush—in Spring City. Oh, how we wanted the piece in Mt. Pleasant! Dad had grown up running equipment, driving trucks, and had some experience in agriculture—he always swore that if he ever purchased land, it would be fertile bottomland. But for some reason, all of us *knew* the property in Mt. Pleasant was not right. The first time Hannah and Leah stepped foot on the acreage in Spring City—ugly though it was—they felt it was home. Before long, the deed for the property was in the Stoddard name.

Though we didn't know why, we felt we were supposed to be there, so we set to work endeavoring to heal this rocky property—making it a refuge for our family. Typical of Dad, he always focused *out*. Dad had a vision for our homestead's ultimate potential, and every family project turned into something that could benefit others. The 11.5 acres would become a retreat for families to disconnect from the chaotic whirlwind of twenty-first century life, walk nature trails, and experience practical self-sufficient living firsthand. We researched which perennial plants would grow in our climate and began transplanting them from all over the world. We put in a pressurized irrigation system so the gardens would be watered on automatic timers, and we brought in load after load of wood chips and leaves to begin naturally amending the soil. We did not use any fertilizers or artificial weed killers. We were going to heal the land naturally using God's laws to restore our new home.

"In This Highland Cathedral of Our God & King"

As the dream began to take shape, we named our homestead Highland Cathedral Estate. "Highland Cathedral" is a famous Scottish song that speaks of being "faithful and loyal" to the "land of our fathers"—rallying Caledonia[1] to be "strong and true" with an "ancient prayer," bearing standards, and petitioning God to restore peace, joy, and liberty "in this Highland Cathedral of our God and King." Not only was our home our own family estate or "cathedral," but as we cleared the land—surrounded by tall, protective, snow-capped mountains— we often wondered whether Nephites had once walked this very property. Eliza R. Snow had spoken of Nephite temples once existing throughout Utah,[2] and according to pioneer Warren S. Snow, President Brigham Young revealed that the ancient prophet Moroni had personally dedicated the site of the Manti, Temple, less than 20 miles from our property:

> We two were alone: President Young took me to the spot where the Temple was to stand; we went to the southeast corner, and President Young said: "Here is the spot where the prophet Moroni stood and dedicated this piece of land for a Temple site, and that is the reason why the location

1   "Caledonia" was the Latin term coined by the Roman Empire for northern Britain and most of Scotland. It is used as a romantic or poetic name for all of Scotland.

2   Eliza R. Snow, "A Journeying Song for the Camp of Israel," *Eliza R. Snow An Immortal* (Salt Lake City: Nicholas G. Morgan, Sr., Foundation, 1957), 267.

is made here, and we can't move it from this spot; and if you and I are the only persons that come here at high noon today, we will dedicate this ground.[3]

Dad could have hired a landscaping team to put in this new enterprise, but Dad knew life was about learning and growing, and we would only learn the necessary skills by doing the work ourselves. So we dug the trenches, we laid the wood chips, we planted thousands and thousands of plants, we worked with him laying the irrigation lines, putting in the septic system, and a host of other tasks!

PRACTICALLY WORKING WITH DAD

Leah remembers: For Dad, investing time was different than calling us out to help him with a job that needed four hands instead of two—finding that it would be too exhausting to do it himself—or just wanting a helper to make the time more enjoyable. No.

The purpose of all this was teaching us new skills that would build our intelligence and character regardless of how it would benefit Dad. He had no ulterior motive—just, how could he help his kids live a happier life?

I remember when my dad first bought our 11.5 acres of property in Sanpete County. He told us many times that he wasn't doing it for himself. Otherwise, he reasoned, he'd just hire a crew to put the place in and be done with it, sipping lemonade on his front porch the next year while gazing over the developed landscape. Instead, we were going to turn it into a family project with perennial gardens that would one day serve other families and bring them closer together—not just us. The first time I stepped on that property, I knew it was a good place.

---

3   Orson F. Whitney, *Life of Heber C. Kimball* (Salt Lake City: Kimball Family, 1888), 447.

Mary attempting to teach her goat how to dance

But I didn't even know what a ratchet was . . . (although I'd been told many times, and that's another story). I'll never forget the first time my dad organized all of our tools inside the large reefer trailer we had parked on the property. The reefer was our temporary "garage" of sorts until we could build a shop. After working for several hours inside the reefer, my dad called me from where I was working and asked me if I wanted to see what it looked like now. I went into the "tools reefer" and found that the entire thing was cleaned spic and span, with heavy-duty shelving lining both sides. Every tool was organized perfectly. All the pipe wrenches were organized from largest to smallest, so, he explained, we could just grab the right wrench when needed. The power tools were on another shelf and the shovels in bins. There was plenty of empty space, so nothing was crammed or shoved together. At that point in time, I had never fathomed how organization really worked—or what it really looked like on a big scale.

Eventually, despite forgetting many times, I also learned to identify the ratchets and sockets.

My dad taught me how to shovel, how to plant, bed and lay pipe, garden, fence, use general tools, etc., but that's not all! His teaching spread to so many areas:

- Scriptures!
- Housekeeping (we have a story about him teaching us the difference between stainless steel and non-stick pans!), cooking, and organization.
- Graphic design and animation
- How to tend babies and little kids
- Coding
- Building
- Speaking/communication
- Dad even built several AR-15 rifles with my brothers, and me. . . even when it may have been easier for him to build them himself. It was a lot of fun!

That took a lot of time and patience for him, I know. There were lots of times when he was tired and just ready to fall over in exhaustion, but he put us before himself, and I respect him for that.

Lessons From Nature

During the 19th and 20th centuries, a smear campaign against agricultural communities began to spread, especially as perpetuated through the media, entertainment, news, and education system. Stereotypes labeling farmers as dirty and uneducated began circulating and children became increasingly ashamed of growing up in 'small towns.' Yet, as we survey the fruits, one cannot help but recognize that the consequences of this rejection have been harmful to families and the development of children. As we were growing up, Dad always had us helping in the yard, laying our own sod, and planting our own garden. When we started Highland Cathedral Estate, we merely expanded our sights to a far broader vision, but the beneficial lessons gained from these experiences are priceless. The following are a few principles that may be helpful for families who are contemplating the essential nature of hard work and agriculture experience in the rearing of any child or family!

Teaches discipline and other essential character traits—In the Book of Mormon, Nephi emphasizes that he specifically taught his people to "build buildings" and to work with a variety of materials including wood, iron, copper, brass, steel, gold, silver, and other metals. He explains that as the leader, he ensured his people were "industrious" and "labor[ed] with their hands." (2 Nephi 5:15, 17) They didn't hire someone else to do their work for them—they rolled up their sleeves, got down in the dirt, and produced their own industry.

Hard work in nature teaches a child how to be disciplined—to push through even when they are tired, hot, and thirsty. The primary weakness of our culture today is discipline. We do not have enough self-control *not* to watch pornography, to say 'no' to inappropriate media, or to restrain ourselves from consuming a plate of brownies. Our children throw temper tantrums, and the thought of controlling one's emotions and natural impulses is a foreign concept no longer taught in our culture at large. An active life in nature, however, gives vigor, it teaches one how to combat difficulties, how to exercise courage, perseverance, and self-control, how to take joy in small and simple things, and become temperate in habits and lifestyle choices.

Far from being a strictly physical exercise, the mind is developed as well. For example, developing soil requires thought, intelligence, creativity, and a thorough understanding of the laws of nature and science to be done correctly. These values then support a child when they turn to their intellectual studies such as math, science, language arts, and business—as they apply this same focus and self-mastery to excel. Labor is noble, honorable, and essential in character development. Our youth should be taught to love hard work!

God designed men and women to labor in nature—The blood of Israel has always been a family culture that inclined to a natural, agrarian lifestyle. Families had estates and farms—space for their children to run and live the way God intended with animals, fresh air, and sunlight, rather than crowded, foul-smelling, air polluted cities. God sent His own Son to the Galilean hills—into a home with self-respecting, hands on, honest labor and economy. The Son of God frequently withdrew from the crowds and cities to go into nature. Joseph Smith was also born into a hardworking, farming family.

Many authors and researchers have commented in the past on the level of crime and the clear decline of morality found in a city lifestyle versus a more country setting. Standards in city life almost always deteriorate and the reason is simple: it is an unnatural lifestyle. Young men were not made to be cooped up in offices and bedrooms—engaging in inefficient and unproductive schooling while being driven to make more money, and chase the next party. In this setting, we must then try to compensate for the lack of physical exercise by creating a complete counterfeit of God's system called a 'gym.' We schedule our memberships and set our New Year's resolutions—forgetting that God already created the best system. Why do we think we know better than Him? God's system develops muscles the *right* way. It is found in a clear and pure environment, and when the laborer is finished, he has produced or created something beneficial to the world—rather than repeating the same isolated movement over and over for a set period of time, leaving the world no better off than when he started. You can tell when a man has developed his so-called strength from the gym, vs. creative, hard-working labor in nature.

These benefits are not for men alone—women *need* this exercise as well! When Adam began "till[ing] the earth" and eating "his bread by the sweat of his brow," Eve was not sitting in the house idling away her time—"And Eve, also, his wife, did labor *with him*." (Moses 5:1)

Our society has attempted to abandon God's natural order in favor of a counterfeit in every detail—artificial foods, artificial love, artificial relationships, artificial exercise, and artificial

Putting in a fire pit and mini-amphitheatre

success. This mimicry breeds idleness and a lack of discipline. Why then are we surprised when the vast majority of men—and even many women now—are addicted to pornography? Or when children become increasingly disrespectful from generation to generation? We have set ourselves up for failure!

Our children need to be prepared for a difficult future—Many inspired leaders have repeatedly warned the Saints that we will not always be able to rely on the convenience of our grocery stores and warehouses. The day will come when we will be left to survive on the food we can produce with our own hands. Do we believe these men? If so, we will take their counsel seriously and prepare our children with the knowledge and skills required to handle any emergency or disaster situation.

 Brigham Young: "We want men to labour [*sic*] in every mechanical pursuit that they can; for I believe that the time will come when we shall have to depend upon our own resources . . ."[4]

---

4 Brigham Young, in *Journal of Discourses*, vol. 7 (Liverpool: Amasa Lyman, 1860), 67.

Heber C. Kimball: "Will you be slack, brethren, and let the evil come upon us, when we forewarn you of the future events that are coming . . . We are telling of what the prophets have said—of what the Lord has said to Joseph. Wake up now, wake up, O Israel, and lay up your grain and your stores. I tell you that there is trouble coming upon the world."[5]

Wilford Woodruff: "The day will come, when, as we have been told, we shall all see the necessity of making our own shoes and clothing and raising our own food."[6]

Spencer W. Kimball: "The little gardens and a few trees are very valuable. I remember when the sisters used to say, 'well, but we could buy it at the store a lot cheaper than we could put it up.' But that isn't quite the answer, is it, Sister Spafford? Because there will become a time when there isn't a store."[7]

Bruce R. McConkie: "I stand before the Church this day and raise the warning voice. . . . It is a voice calling upon the Lord's people to prepare for the troubles and desolations which are about to be poured out upon the world without measure. For the moment we live in a day of peace and prosperity but it shall not ever be thus. Great trials lie ahead. All of the sorrows and perils of the past are but a foretaste of what is yet to be. And we must prepare ourselves temporally and spiritually."[8]

---

5   Heber C. Kimball, in *Journal of Discourses*, vol. 4 (Liverpool: S. W. Richards, 1857), 336-339.

6   Wilford Woodruff, *The Discourses of Wilford Woodruff*, ed. G. Homer Durham (Bookcraft, 1946), 166.

7   Spencer W. Kimball, *General Conference*, April 1974.

8   Bruce R. McConkie, *Ensign*, May 1979, 92-93.

Gordon B. Hinckley: "We feel the need to emphasize with greater clarity the obligation for members of the Church to become more independent and self reliant."[9]

God teaches through nature—The body and mind are connected—to maintain the body is to strengthen the spirit. The laws God placed in the natural earth mirror the laws operating in the spiritual world—indeed, the Lord does not recognize any difference between the two! It is Godlike to create and establish order. Through physical, hands-on labor we learn we are capable of accomplishing far more than we realize, and the spiritual insights that come while working in nature are often profound.

FINDING GOD'S PURPOSE FOR SUFFERING IN GOAT DISBUDDING

Hannah remembers: I believe God intended us to work in nature because we learn about Him by harmonizing with the world/system He created.

Each spring, a few days after their birth, each baby goat has to be 'disbudded.' This process involves taking a hot iron and burning the newly forming horns or 'buds.' If allowed to grow, the horns can pose life-threatening problems. Goat's horns can become caught in a fence, leaving them susceptible to dying from dehydration. Their horns can also endanger other goats through fighting or even killing one another, and this presents obvious danger to humans as well.

The first time I disbudded one of our goats I was overwhelmed with a spiritual lesson. I felt my heart being torn apart having to bind down one of these perfect, innocent baby animals—who never did me any harm— and apply scalding, searing pain to its head. The baby's eyes seemed to plead with me in confusion, "*I thought you were my friend? I thought you were supposed to help*

---

9 Gordon B. Hinckley, *General Conference*, April 1983.

me?" As I saw them writhing in pain during the procedure, I almost felt to doubt myself. How could I inflict this pain?

In a moment, a healing understanding washed over me of God's perspective toward *us.* How many times had I looked at God and asked, "How could you allow this suffering? I laid down my life to serve you! I sacrificed my mind, heart, talents, dreams, and hopes to follow you. Why are you allowing this pain?" I'm not speaking of pain that comes from sin, but afflictions, persecutions, and suffering as a follower of Christ.

Suddenly, I could see God with the iron as we finished the disbudding process. This precious little baby did not understand that we were doing this for his/her own good, or that in order to secure their future, it was better this way. I deliberately placed the iron on the head—I inflicted this pain out of LOVE.

If we feel a spirit that communicates self-pity or complaint because of difficulty, let us remember that this is NOT the fruit of the spirit of God. If we want to become like God, we must eventually suffer, endure and overcome all things. The path of a true Christian is always marked with sacrifice and tribulation; however:

> [B]lessed is he that keepeth my commandments, whether in life or in death; and he that is faithful in tribulation, the reward of the same is greater in the kingdom of heaven.

> Ye cannot behold with your natural eyes, for the present time, the design of your God concerning those things which shall come hereafter, and the glory which shall follow after much tribulation.

> For after much tribulation come the blessings . . . for this cause I have sent you—that you might be obedient, and that your hearts might be prepared to bear testimony of

Leaves, leaves, leaves!

the things which are to come . . . (Doctrine & Covenants 58:2-6)

If we keep the faith, it will all be worth it in the end.

Miracles

No lie—a *lot* of work went into Highland Cathedral. Long days in all weather and all seasons—planting, harvesting, weeding, and putting in new infrastructure to support the ultimate project. Shortly after buying the property, a neighbor began complaining about the old fence that was there from the previous owners. We hadn't yet found the time to replace it, but the neighbor demanded we fix it at once. So we went down to Spring City, between snowstorms, to fix the border. Another year, we planted over one thousand trees, shrubs, herbs and other plants in the space of a few weeks! That was *insane*. We learned quickly how to think on our feet, to push ourselves when we wanted to give up, and the reality that nothing good can come without a *lot* of effort and sacrifice. At the same time, like our documentaries and books, we realized that without the Lord's help, we would surely fail.

DROUGHT MIRACLE

Leah remembers: In July of 2018, Spring City experienced its worst drought in over 50 years. We were completely unaware that water would be scarce that year, and had felt prompted to buy and plant over 2,000 berries, trees and herbal plants from all around the world. We had just finished and Dad had announced, "Time to celebrate!" We laughed and planned a season of relaxation as we drove down to our property the next Saturday, but when we arrived, Dad went over to a frost-free hydrant, pulled up the handle and . . . no water came out. Had a pipe burst? When we couldn't diagnose the problem, Dad called the local water master.

"Oh, the water is off," came the simple response.

"Ummm, when do you think it will be turned on?"

"We have no idea. This year is the worst drought we've had in over fifty years. Could be days—or weeks. It could even be a month or two. See the mountain? [Our irrigation water came from snow melting off the mountain] There's no more snow up there. No melting snow, no water. If we're lucky, we may be able to pull in extra water from some ponds in a few weeks. But right now, there's no water."

A month or two! No water? We were in shock. We had just worked our tails off for several months to prep the ground and plant thousands of little plants all over the property. If we didn't get water within a day or two, they would all be dead—and the July heat wasn't helping.

Our drinking well was the only water source, so we got out buckets and went to work hand watering acres of plants. We tried connecting garden hoses and stretching them all across the property. But there wasn't enough water pressure and there were too many plants. We were afraid to keep the well running for long because we were afraid the motor would overheat and break. We were pretty much relegated to pioneer status—kids carrying buckets. This went on for weeks—the situation looked grim. Conversations at the dinner table, over lunch, on walks, and while driving in the car began revolving around the weather.

There was no forecast for rain, but one day, we were working in the vineyard when Dad gathered us and said he felt we needed to pray. We got down on our knees right there on our property and pleaded with the Lord for rain. The sky was perfectly blue but suddenly, within a short time, clouds came out of nowhere and rain began falling right over Spring City. However, it only sprinkled for a few minutes and then stopped. Dad looked quizzically up at the sky. "I think we were picturing a little more than that," he jokingly told the Lord.

It rained a little in the night but the ground was still mostly dry. Dad commented that the Lord might be testing our faith. Sure enough, it rained a week later. It rained more than it had the *entire year*. Several inches of water. In the middle of July. Unheard of.

Needless to say, we all got on our knees right away and gave a prayer of gratitude and thanksgiving, and any time it has rained since then, we've always been grateful and reminded of this miracle.

MIRACLE FIXING THE EXCAVATOR

Hannah remembers: I have a miracle recorded in my journal from July 2015, a little over a year after first purchasing our property in Spring City, UT. God's miracles do not always have to be grand "Red Sea partings." Sometimes they are small and simple, but to the recipients, they are life changing. My entry reads (with a few minor edits):

"A little under three weeks ago, I went down with Dad to Spring City. While there, we were attempting to fix an issue with the engine. My dad did not know how to fix the issue and was on the cell phone repeatedly with a man (who sells or rents equipment). The first miracle was that we are able to make progress at all. Phone calls and driving down the street to send snapshot pictures through our tablet is not efficient communication. Then came a point where Dad was tightening a screw back on and could not get it to tighten. We were struck with sudden fear that the nut had been stripped. After being unable to tighten it, we called the gentleman helping us, and he said it WAS likely stripped, and we needed to replace the nut. Isaiah and I ran to the reefer where we kept our tools and got as many of our random buckets of nuts as we could find, and we started going through them. Unfortunately we could not find the right size. After several long minutes, Dad finally said 'we are going to have to go to stores for the rest of today and try to find the right size.' We had so much to get done, and we didn't have time to waste running around the valley to get the hardware we needed! During the entire ordeal, I know I was mentally praying hard. Suddenly, Isaiah miraculously found a bag of nuts, we opened the bag, and lo and behold the exact size was in there. An hour later, the excavator was going! Dad turned to me and said, 'This is because of all your praying.' It was a complete miracle!"

Priceless Blessings

While there were several times we grumbled as we dragged on our socks and boots, we are eternally grateful that Dad recognized the essential nature of hands on labor, and made the sacrifices necessary to purchase and build the first phase of Highland Cathedral Estate. The development of our character, the health benefits, the food and produce provided, the opportunities for bonding, and the many uplifting laughs and tears experienced on our homestead have made us the men and women we are today.

CHAPTER
Ten

POWER COMES FROM PURITY

*"If you wish to go where God is, you must be like God . . .
Search your hearts, and see if you are like God. I have
searched mine, and feel to repent of all my sins."*

— *Joseph Smith*[1]

When Dad was on his mission, he was often assigned to work with many of the struggling elders. There were periods when he would tract all day, only to return and be forced to stay awake for hours in the night, listening to his companion flirting with his girlfriend on the phone. The mission president had specifically set up their companionship because he trusted Dad to report back to him everything going on. Needless to say, he gained a lot of life experience on his mission.

One day, Dad drove to visit some missionaries who were staying in an apartment complex after complaints had been called in regarding some of their behavior. As he pulled into the parking lot, he was concerned to hear AC/DC music blaring loudly. *"This is not a good environment for missionaries,"* he thought. *"No wonder we are having problems."*

---

1   Joseph Smith, History, 1838–1856, volume C-1 Addenda, p. 62, The Joseph Smith Papers.

His concern changed to alarm when he realized the music was coming from the *missionaries'* apartment. When he walked in their door, he gasped at the sight before him. A full on rock band was set up with huge posters of movie stars, rock artists, and girlfriends covering the walls. In the middle of one wall stood a lonely picture of the Savior.

The missionaries panicked when they saw Elder Stoddard walk in and waited uncomfortably for what was coming next. Dad didn't say much as he glanced about the room. Finally, he took a deep breath. "You know what elders? I'm cool with this, but I just have one problem."

"What's that, Elder Stoddard?" one of them responded.

"*That!*" he said emphatically, pointing to the picture of Jesus Christ on the wall. "You can keep the rest, but that picture *must* come down."

With that, Dad walked out of the room, having made his point. He didn't care how people wanted to live, but pretending to follow Christ, while living like Babylon, was hypocrisy. Just be true to who you *really* are, and what you *really* believe. Make the decision to choose the Lord or Baal.

Are You Comfortable With the Culture?

"The Lord has told us that we live at the most wicked time on the most wicked earth. In other words, if we feel comfortable or at ease with the modernist culture (movies, music, diet, fashion, language, literature, parenting philosophies, schools, etc.), we must think again. *This is not who you really are.*"

We grew up hearing Dad make this thought-provoking comment during family scripture study, to families who came for counsel and advice, to neighbors who wanted to know why our family was 'different,' and many other friends who came and went through the years.

Dad helped family after family—individual after individual—find new life and hope after cleaning up their entertainment, lifestyle, movies, music, and so forth. Men and women who were lost or who struggled with receiving revelation suddenly began experiencing the windows of heaven open. Dad knew what it was like to grow up in the culture. He knew what it was like to feel as though he was a wanderer. For years, he used the username "lone pilgrim," revealing his search for his true people and home. He wanted *more*. When he discovered his true identity, he just wanted others to experience that same peace and joy. This was the message Dad passed on to his kids:

1. **You are of the blood of Israel.** The blood of Israel longs for a culture of refinement, beauty, purity, honor, and integrity. Live up to your birthright.

2. **Power comes from purity.** You cannot do the work of the Lord without living righteously. The good you do in the world will correspond to your righteousness.

3. **Jesus Christ is the Exemplar.** Do not look to the world or any mortal man for the ultimate standard of holiness. Your standard is Jesus Christ, the Master. Seek to be like Him.

4. **Stand as a Witness.** Never be ashamed of who you are and spread the light and goodness that comes from pure living with others.

Living Up to Your True Identity

Have you ever felt lost? Like you didn't know where you belonged? Like there was something more—a place that your heart would recognize as *your* home, with family you knew were *your* people, serving *your* God? Like you were searching for your place, but you didn't know where to find it?

A fictional allegory is told of a young noble prince, an heir, who was cruelly snatched from his rightful home, his parents, his family, his culture—everything that was familiar and secure—and relocated to the lone and dreary enemy territory. As the story goes:

 . . . the prince was taken by those who dethroned the king. They thought that inasmuch as the king's son was heir to the throne, if they could destroy him morally, he would never realize the great and grand destiny that life had bestowed upon him.

They took him to a community far away, and there they exposed the lad to every filthy and vile thing that life could offer. They exposed him to foods the richness of which would quickly make him a slave to appetite. They used vile language around him constantly. They exposed him to lewd and lusting women. They exposed him to dishonor and distrust. He was surrounded 24 hours a day by everything that could drag the soul of a man as low as one could slip. For over six months he had this treatment— but not once did the young lad buckle under pressure. Finally, after intensive temptation, they questioned him. Why had he not submitted himself to these things— why had he not partaken? These things would provide pleasure, satisfy his lusts, and were desirable; they were all his. The boy said, "I cannot do what you ask for I was born to be a king."[2]

---

2   Vaughn J. Featherstone, "The King's Son," *New Era*, November 1975.

The young prince stood firm because he knew who he was! Dad likewise taught us that we were Latter-day Israel; we were the sons and daughters of righteous men and women who stood for truth throughout the centuries. Around 2009, Dad wrote Hannah a letter emphasizing this message. She was 14 years old and about to go on Trek with our stake. Parents were invited to write a letter to their youth, and Dad's letter read as follows:

 Dear Hannah,

I feel it is a great privilege and blessing to be able to write this letter. . . . Thank you for the work that you perform on behalf of the family. As you grow older you will not care how many parties or activities that you attended, but only how well you served the Lord, your family and others. Thank you for your desire to live the commandments of God and to excel in your education. As you faithfully work to acquire knowledge that can be used in the service of the Lord you will find the Lord guiding you in the path of true happiness. Remember to stay pure and be reverent. The adversary desires to take away your happiness. He can only do this by tempting you to be unclean or lulling you to become complacent or disrespectful of sacred things. In the Lord's presence there is no grey, no unkindness, and no thought of self. His love cannot be comprehended by anything in this world. There is no sacrifice too great, no obstacle too immense and no commandment too difficult in this pursuit. All other considerations in this life are as but dross in seeking His Face. This I know with surety. Have the courage to stand for what you believe and do what you know is true. If you are ever alone, be worthy and He will come to you. Remember the Lord is the Rock that you must build upon. Trust His words in your study, trust His comfort in your pain and trust His Arm in your defense. There is no other unfaltering friend.

At this time remember that you have the blood of prophets and martyrs in your veins. Your ancestors gave us this country, helped to restore the true Church and have defended the Faith of the Fathers. They founded the first and greatest settlements both in this country and in the Church. They defended and led armies in the protection of this nation and this Gospel. They quietly mourned and moved on as their loved ones died in the Cause of Christ. They have suffered and bled; and can we expect less. Serve the Lord, as they have done, with all of your heart, might, mind and strength. . . . You are a daughter of our Father in heaven as well as His Son. Your joys are His joys, your tears are His tears, and your success will come from following Him in all things. Without His aid, you cannot succeed; with His assistance you cannot fail. If you will give Him all that you have; He will give you all that He has.

Love, Dad

What are the Fruits?

While Dad held our standards high, he wasn't doing so as the party-pooper, killjoy tyrant who hates to hear children laughing and singing. Quite the opposite! Dad was the one who taught us that balance and leisure are essential. Although we would all agree he pushed *himself* way too hard—driven by a weight to accomplish his mission in the limited time span he had—he kept reminding us that the purpose of life is *joy!* Emotion is a gift from God. We aren't purging all passion and happiness—we are searching for everything that is refined, noble, honest, and virtuous. Why? Because power comes from purity. If you want to be great, you must be good and the fruits speak for themselves.

SUCCESSFULLY RESISTING PORNOGRAPHY

Isaiah remembers: Today, many people think that looking at pornography is normal and that everyone does it. They say it can't be avoided, and that it's impossible to grow up without wanting to do it. People who say they haven't done it are viewed as weird and are accused of lying. I disagree with that attitude. I believe that I was shielded from pornography by eliminating rock music with inappropriate beats, keeping my standards high in movies, and following other commandments. I have always considered pornography to be disgusting, and I have never voluntarily viewed it. And I am certain that the same can happen to you.

Many people will often use technology to try to prevent their children from being exposed to pornography. The problem is that it's everywhere. The exposure will happen eventually—no matter how hard we attempt to monitor and prevent it. The question is, are we going to try everything else before we turn to the Lord for help? My Dad would often remind us that the Gospel is about helping people have joy and allowing them to think for themselves—not turn them into micromanaged robots.

The real answer that worked for me was not through force or isolation, but through the gospel of Jesus Christ and giving up what I want to do for what He wants me to do. It's not easy to make that decision, but it can't be done any other way. Satan is much more crafty and deceptive than we can possibly understand, and there is no middle ground. We can't follow the world and then expect to not reap the side effects. We can't keep our worldly movies, music, and video games and then imagine that we won't be attracted to other sinful things like pornography. We either follow Christ and his commandments or we take the easy path and follow Lucifer (3 Nephi 13:24). We have to experience for ourselves the change of heart that the people of King Benjamin felt which caused them to have "no more disposition to do evil, but to do good continually."(Mosiah 5:2) The time to decide was yesterday. If we go into battle half-willed and undecided which side we are on, then we will fail.

The scriptures give us the key to resisting the temptations of Satan effectively. In the Book of Mormon, as Nephi is interpreting his father's vision of the tree of life to his brothers, he explains that the iron rod is a representation of the word of God, and that: "whoso would hearken unto the word of God, and would hold fast unto it, they would never perish; neither could the temptations and the fiery darts of the adversary overpower them unto blindness, to lead them away to destruction." (1 Nephi 15:24)

There is a way to successfully resist Satan. It's not a maybe, or a "try as best as you can," but a firm *yes.* Sin should be the abnormal instead of the 'normal.' It's not a complicated process and it doesn't involve any special program that you have to follow—but it does involve the gospel of Jesus Christ.

Once you make the decision to follow the Son of God, expect fierce opposition. Everyone who becomes a real

Christian is placed on Satan's 'most wanted list.' Satan knows all of our weaknesses and he knows that it only takes one crack in our foundation for us to become compromised. In 2015, the wall of an irrigation canal in a nearby city to where we lived suddenly gave way and within a few minutes, hundreds of gallons of water began pouring down the side of a hill. It was later determined that the flood had been started by a gopher that had burrowed a tiny hole into the canal which had caused the wall to quickly erode. Like that tiny hole, if we are not constantly vigilant in watching for the little things, they will quickly destroy us. King Benjamin warns us that:

> If ye do not watch yourselves, and your thoughts, and your words, and your deeds, and observe the commandments of God, and continue in the faith of what ye have heard concerning the coming of our Lord, even unto the end of your lives, ye must perish. And now, O man, remember, and perish not. (Mosiah 4:30)

The promises of protection in the scriptures are there. We have the agency to decide which path we will go down. (Doctrine & Covenants 58:28) I've personally seen the difference that the gospel of Jesus Christ can make. It doesn't just strengthen our foundation, it is the foundation. Helaman tells us that "it is upon the rock of our Redeemer, who is Christ, the Son of God, that ye must build your foundation." If we do this, the promise is clear that:

> . . . when the devil shall send forth his mighty winds, yea, his shafts in the whirlwind, yea, when all his hail and his mighty storm shall beat upon you, it shall have no power over you to drag you down to the gulf of misery and endless wo, because of the rock upon which ye are built, which is a sure foundation, a foundation whereon if men build they cannot fall. (Helaman 5:12)

If you want to be able to successfully resist the temptations of pornography, the only way that will ultimately work is to be born again. It has to come from the inside. You will only know this if you try it for yourself.

REVELATION & MIRACLES CAME FROM LIVING STANDARDS

Hannah remembers: I was once asked whether I really believed our family lifestyle influenced what we accomplished. I know firsthand that it is the standards and the lifestyle that have made *the* difference. I know with absolute certainty that Presidents Harold B. Lee, Ezra Taft Benson and other leaders were inspired by their counsel on music. They didn't have the scientific "evidence" at the time—now that is starting to be discovered—but they had the Spirit.

I know without the smallest shadow of doubt that there is *no physical way on earth* that logically our family should have been able to accomplish what we have done in the last 17 years (dating from the beginning of ZionVision in 2005). I spent a significant portion of my life growing up flat on my back in bed from some inherited health issues, we moved multiple times, juggled little kids, maintained homeschooling for nine children, and my Dad worked full time. In other words, there were a *lot* of odds not in our favor. Our family isn't just "lucky"—any other family could do it. The biggest mistakes in my life, my lowest points, and greatest errors in discernment coincided with times when I didn't live up to the standards I knew in my heart were correct. At the same time, the greatest miracles and moments of true revelation in my life have come when I *was* living pure. This is not an accident!

One of the biggest motivations for me to "experiment on the word" and gain my own testimony of higher standards was from watching my Dad's example. When

he gave Priesthood blessings, he didn't ramble his own thoughts. Each word was given slowly, carefully, and precisely. And the blessings came to pass with astonishing accuracy! Many times he expressed thoughts and counsel that answered questions *no one on earth* knew I had! Only the Lord. When we were writing books, inspiration would come as he dictated chapters and strategized future projects. I witnessed it often. It takes a *lot* of responsibility to oversee a family mission. Receiving revelation is not easy; it requires work and you have to be right every time. If you are wrong, your family cannot place the trust and respect in your leadership.

Dad was inspired because he lived *good*. He wasn't perfect—I knew his flaws better than perhaps anyone—but he apologized when he made a mistake and he did everything humanly possible to choose the right path. And I saw the results! I *know* because I personally witnessed the fruits of a man who lived pure, and God blessed him for it. Dad wasn't 'special' or 'lucky,' he was just a man. But

> he made choices that allowed him to be chosen, instead of just called. (Doctrine & Covenants 121:34-35)
>
> No culture change is easy; in fact, I think it is one of the *hardest* things and one of the greatest tests of character—revealing who we really are inside—but it is worth it!

To Whom Shall We Go?

The question naturally follows: how do we weigh where and how we should change our standards? Do we recreate a past decade or era? Do we copy another family? All of these methods fall short—they are simply relying on the arm of flesh, and Nephi warned this would only bring a curse in the end (2 Nephi 4:34).

Many often refer to Jesus Christ as the "Savior," but Dad always preferred the title, "the Master." In one of his many sets of scriptures, he has a note scribbled off to the side of Doctrine & Covenants 50. "Some think there are a certain number of commandments (i.e. 1,000 or 1,000,000, etc.) This is the wrong attitude. The standard is Jesus Christ. If we are not like Him, we must repent." That was Dad's standard in life. Jesus Christ was his exemplar, his prototype, his "Master." He just wanted to be like *Him*. Would He watch this movie? No? Then don't watch it. Would He listen to this music? Yes? Then play it!

Dad knew the Lord had the answers found through prayerful study of the scriptures and inspired words of latter-day prophets—coupled with inspiration, study, and obedience. From this search for truth, principles could be found to apply in our daily lives—not rules, not formulas, not cultural customs, and not memorized regulations. Principles were the answer. The following two chapters, *Music: The Forgotten Language of the Heart* and *Our Philosophy on Movies* were written by our Dad, sharing his testimony and the principles he encouraged in his children's lives. We know without a shadow of a doubt that these principles *work!* We hope they can be a benefit and blessing as you seek to study and implement higher standards in your own home.

CHAPTER
Eleven

MUSIC: THE FORGOTTEN
LANGUAGE OF THE HEART

"For my soul delighteth in the song of the heart; yea, the song of the righteous is a prayer unto me . . ."

— Doctrine & Covenants 25:12

Originally published by James F. Stoddard III on the Joseph Smith Foundation website. Reprinted here with minor edits.

I believe that *every* feeling, every emotion that can be felt by man, can be expressed through music. Can it be that while we have been immersed in this medium, we have been seduced and distracted to forget its power for good or evil?

My story with music begins when I was very young. This was the age long before CDs or MP3 players. This was the age of the radio and a few cassettes. About age seven or eight, I can remember feeling strongly that the spirit accompanying the popular music of the day (the late 70s, early 80s) was corrupt. I am not referring to the words or lyrics, but the music itself. I could sense that the pop songs played on the radio were dangerous–some dark, others irreverent and still others anxious.

As I grew older, the near universal sentiment was opposed to such notions. Teachers and religious leaders often promoted the music and were strongly in favor of such entertainment. To a young child, and later to a young adult, this was utterly confusing. I would like to reiterate that these impressions were NOT connected with the lyrics of these popular tunes. This inspiration was warning me of a more subtle communicator: the beat, rhythm and other dynamics of the composition itself. This perplexity, almost smothered, continued in the back of my mind until I returned home from my mission in 1991. Having a very inquiring mind, and some strong promptings, I took my questions back off the shelf and began searching for answers. I wanted to know if the leadership of the Church had spoken on this subject and if they had, what had they said? Thus began an extraordinary journey.

"Issues with Answers"

Being an extremely impoverished college student, I was looking through the religious and prophetically oriented books at Deseret Industries, and I happened to see a CES Church manual, "*Living Prophets for a Living Church*," 1974. Thumbing through, I found a section titled "Issues with Answers." Skimming quickly, I noticed matter-of-fact statements about the civil rights movement, working mothers, birth control, socialism, overpopulation, sex education, and finally, music and dance. Among my first discoveries was President David O. McKay's advice to BYU students: no "electronic bands" and no "loud beat."

 A feeling of the brethren on dancing for The Church of Jesus Christ of Latter-day Saints has been received in a letter to a BYU student from President David O. McKay. President McKay said in his letter that one copy had been sent to President Ernest L. Wilkinson [President of BYU] and authorized Miss Chandler to show it 'to anyone you desire.' 'I am answering your letter because it raises a question on which I desire all youth of the Church to know my views.' THE DAILY UNIVERSE received permission from Miss Chandler to print the letter in its entirety, so that all BYU students will know how the President of the

Church feels about the dance issue. 'THE STANDARDS of acceptable dancing for the young men and women of our Church are being set forth in a revised booklet entitled 'For the Strength of the Youth.' [not the current *For the Strength of Youth* manual] This little booklet, as soon as it comes off the press, will contain the statement which I am enclosing herewith. I note you say that you enjoy what you characterize as 'stomp dances,' [the fast dance of the 1970s and 1980s that became popular at stake dances in my generation, as opposed to the waltz or two-step] but you are willing to follow my counsel no matter what the answer. I congratulate you on this attitude. You also say that many people have no evil intentions in dancing these dances. May I give you the following guidelines in reply:

1. THE ENCLOSED statement of acceptable dancing states that if one concentrates on good dance posture, many dances can be danced in a manner which will meet LDS standards. Examples of these dances are the waltz, the fox trot, tango, rhumba, cha-cha, samba, and the swing, and most of the folk dances, for which the Brigham Young University has a very wholesome and fine reputation. The seven dances which I have enumerated have all been approved by the General Boards of the Mutual Improvement Associations. This should provide a sufficient variety of dances to enable the youth of Zion to have a good time.

2. YOU ENCLOSED with your letter a photograph appearing in the Daily Universe of an off-campus 'stomp' dance. I do not believe that those photographed in that picture are concentrating on good posture. Indeed, I doubt whether it is possible to dance most of the prevalent fad dances in a manner that will meet LDS standards, and I know that is why President Wilkinson, who has the complete support of the Board of Trustees, criticized certain dances in his address to the student body. The standards which he outlined for BYU are standards approved by the General Authorities.

3. I admit that many of the young people of our Church do not have any evil intentions in dancing certain current fad dances. However, we do not think the test of a proper dance is whether the dancers have evil intentions, but whether the dance is of such dignity and propriety that, even to an onlooker, it suggests nothing but style and good grace. AFTER ALL, young men and women of our Church should shun even the appearance of evil, and that is why we would very much prefer that you and others avoid the current trend of what, to many of us, appears to be vulgar dancing [the dancing that became the standard in my era]. There are too many fine things in this world for the young people to engage in without resorting to dances that are questionable.

4. You inquired as to what is wrong with electronic bands. I am informed that moderate and modest music can be played by electronic bands, but I also understand that most electronic bands have a very loud beat which is inconsistent with the standards we desire to have observed; also, that in some places, two bands are employed because the traditional band or orchestra is not satisfactory for the wild and loud beat necessary for certain fad dances. That is why, in general, electronic bands are not approved.

'I HOPE THAT you and your friends will follow my advice by dancing in accordance with the standards. You will find that when you accept those standards [these standards were rejected and forgotten by my day] you will get much more joy and wholesome satisfaction than you do from the questionable dancing engaged in by many [nearly everyone since then], and you will not be in an atmosphere where there is smoking or drinking as described by you in one of the places where you dance.'[1]

---

1   David O. McKay, as printed in the *Daily Universe*, December 3, 1965, 1-2; *Living Prophets for a Living Church*, Church Educational System college student manual, 1974.

As I began to study, I realized that the timing of President McKay's statements coincided with my own parent's association with BYU. I approached my mother to discover a forgotten history of music standards as advised by the Church. My mother explained that she had grown up with a very different style of music. Again, we were discussing music, NOT LYRICS. As time progressed through the 50s, the 60s, and then the 70s and 80s, the music became harder and harder and louder and louder. President David O. McKay and President Ernest L. Wilkinson, BYU President from 1951-1971, were adamantly opposed to introducing this new popular music and dancing onto the campus. The BYU student body of that time, unfortunately, did not follow the counsel. Because the generations preceding my own had rejected the counsel of the Prophet in regard to rock music, my generation never had the chance to be taught a higher standard. I felt like the prophet Josiah when he first discovered the forgotten Book of the Law. My disappointment in having never heard this narrative before was keen. Such advice and instruction could have benefited my early life, but I was now determined that even if I stood alone, I would stand. After pouring through my personal music collection, albums nearly everyone would have considered extremely tame, I discarded the majority. I struggled to develop a taste for a higher standard of music; a taste for compositions that were more pure and holy. Bit by bit and piece by piece, I began to understand more clearly why the Presidents of the Church had given their counsel. This set me on a crusade. I poured through the teachings of the Presidents of the Church, and before long my understanding of music was revolutionized. Here is a sampling:

President Benson

 Have you been listening to the music that many young folks are hearing today? Some of it is nerve-jamming in nature and much of it has been deliberately designed to promote revolution, dope, immorality, and a gap between parent and child. And some of this music has invaded our Church cultural halls. Have you noticed some of our Church dances lately? Have they been praiseworthy, lovely, and of good report? (Article of Faith 13) "I doubt," said President David O. McKay, "whether it is possible to dance most of the prevalent fad dances in a manner to meet LDS standards."[2]

Youth leaders, are you holding aloft our standards, or have you compromised them for the lowest common denominator in order to appease the deceived or vile within the Church? Are the dances and music in your cultural halls virtuous, lovely, praiseworthy, and of good report, or do they represent a modern Sodom with short skirts, loud beat, strobe lights, and darkness? . . . Have we, as Moroni warned, "polluted the holy church of God"? The auxiliaries of the Church are to be a help, not a hindrance, to parents and the priesthood as they strive to lead their families back to God. . . .Today because some parents have refused to become informed and then stand up and inform their children, they are witnessing the gradual physical and spiritual destruction of their posterity. If we would become like God, knowing good and evil, then we had best find out what is undermining us, how to avoid it, and what we can do about it.[3]

President Packer

In our day music itself has been corrupted. Music can, by its tempo, by its beat, by its intensity, dull the spiritual sensitivity of men. . . .

---

2   Ezra Taft Benson, *The Teachings of Ezra Taft Benson* (Salt Lake City: Bookcraft, 1988), 325.

3   Ezra Taft Benson, *God, Family, Country: Our Three Great Loyalties* (Salt Lake City: Deseret Book Co., 1974), 229.

One of the signs of apostasy in the Christian churches today is the willingness of their ministers to compromise and introduce into what had been, theretofore, the most sacred religious meetings the music of the drug and the hard rock culture. Such music has little virtue and it is repellent to the Spirit of God. . . .

Someone said recently that no music could be degrading, that music in and of itself is harmless and innocent.

If that be true, then there should be some explanation for circumstances where local leaders have provided a building—expansive, light, and inviting—and have assembled a party of young people dressed modestly, well-groomed, with manners to match. Then over amplified sounds of hard music are introduced and an influence pours into the room that is repellent to the Spirit of God.

. . . we have not given sufficient counsel and attention, I think, to the music that our young people consume. And "consume" is a proper word. . . .

. . . the breach between the world and the extremes of its music and the Church is wider in our day than ever in generations past.[4]

President Harold B. Lee

At the same time music can be prostituted to Satan's purposes. Napoleon is quoted as having said, "Music of all the liberal arts has the greatest influence over the passions and is that which the legislator ought to give the greatest encouragement." May I paraphrase and say, "Music in the Church of Jesus Christ is that to which every leader of youth should give his greatest

---

4 Boyd K. Packer, "Inspiring Music–Worthy Thoughts," *Ensign*, October 1973.

concern to see that the wrong kinds of passions are not aroused by our introduction of sensuous music into our youth programs.[5]

We're winged for heavenly flight. Have you ever gone out to a bonfire party late at night? As you build the bonfire you see moths come winging in around the fire, and if they get too close they fall singed to their death, or if they're able to fly away they're maimed forever after. That's exactly what you have in life. The hellholes of Satan are always made very attractive. [They feature] enticing music of the kind that appeals to the lower senses. Now, there may be good rock music—I don't know what it is— but there's damnable rock music that appeals to the lower senses of man, where the offbeat [rock beat] is just as vile and abrasive to human thought as it can be. We say it to you, we plead with you to listen to the beautiful things, if you want to be on the right side. But be careful you don't choose the wrong things; you shun those things just as the moths should have shunned the white fire.[6]

President Spencer W. Kimball

 Musical sounds can be put together in such a way that they can express feelings—from the most profoundly exalted to the most abjectly vulgar. Or rather, these musical sounds induce in the listener feelings which he responds to, and the response he makes to these sounds has been called a "gesture of the spirit." Thus, music can act upon our senses to produce or induce feelings of reverence, humility, fervor, assurance, or other feelings attuned to the spirit of worship.[7]

5   Harold B. Lee, *The Teachings of Harold B. Lee*, ed. by Clyde J. Williams (Salt Lake City: Bookcraft, 1996), 203.

6   Ibid., 104.

7   Spencer W. Kimball, *The Teachings of Spencer W. Kimball*, ed. by Edward L. Kimball (Salt Lake City: Bookcraft, 1982), 519.

Note: For an exhaustive list of statements made by the LDS Church leadership please see the Joseph Smith Foundation Music & Dance FAQs.

As has been the case with the advice of the Brethren on politics[8], education[9], birth-control[10] and science[11], the majority of the student body and faculty of BYU from time to time has opposed the advice and teachings of the Prophets of God. As I avoided these modern forms of music, I began to understand, I began to more clearly see that music imitated emotion or feeling. Before long I recognized that hard rock generally imitated feelings of anger or frustration in varying degrees. As I did not desire to be consumed in animosity, it was an easy decision to steer clear of that genre (I had never liked it). Soon thereafter, "pop rock" also became unmasked, and I began to see imitations of pride and arrogance. In other words, the music, not the words but the music itself, imitates or expresses or conveys feelings of pride and arrogance. Modern music also has a near universal influence on the mind and the body to "just be free to do what it feels like."

There was, however, one genre that still remained a mystery to me. Elder Gene R. Cook made the following comment in regard to the standard for music in his own home. "We determined to maintain our family music standard of Church music, classical music, or other good general music, but no light or hard rock or

---

8   See the Joseph Smith Foundation Government FAQs.

9   "Traditions of Scholarship that Shape the Foundations of Education and the Nature of the University," by Neil J. Flinders.

10   See the Joseph Smith Foundation Home & Family FAQs: "01) BIRTH-CONTROL: What is the first commandment ever given by the Lord to man? How does the Lord feel about birth control? Should couples postpone having children?"

11   See the Joseph Smith Foundation Science FAQS: "13) 3 BYU PROFESSORS: Why did President Joseph F. Smith dismiss three professors from Brigham Young University for teaching organic evolution?"

anything like unto it."[12] I could understand the danger of hard rock, imitating anger or contention or anxiety, but what threat did light or soft rock have? What could be the problem with a very light rock beat in the background? Or what could be wrong with light music with no rock beat (off beat) at all? Though I did not understand it at the time, I knew I should follow the counsel. Years later, the lights went on; I had an epiphany of sorts. Music communicates emotion, feeling. Hard rock generally conveys anger; pop rock relays pride and arrogance, but soft rock was sinister as it imitated feelings of lust or looseness and letting go. I realized more and more that all rock music, soft, pop, hard, etc. promoted the natural man to a greater or lesser degree. Was this music the adversary's counterfeit to spiritual communication with the heart?

Doctrine & Covenants 8:2 — The Mind and Heart

God communicates with His children in two ways according to scripture. When the Lord taught Oliver Cowdery how to receive revelation, he was perfectly instructed:

> I will tell you in your mind and in your heart, by the Holy Ghost, which shall come upon you and which shall dwell in your heart. (Doctrine & Covenants 8:2)

We should ask ourselves, what is the language of the mind? With some reflection, it becomes apparent that the conveying medium of the mind is words. For many of us, English is the medium we use to describe the workings of the mind or that we employ to impart intellectual concepts. All written and spoken languages, mathematics, computer languages, etc. could be considered languages of the mind. This begs the question, what then is the language of the heart? What is the heart? The heart is feeling and emotion. Webster's 1828 Dictionary defines the heart as "the seat of the affections and passions."

---

12 Gene R. Cook, *Raising Up a Family to the Lord* (Deseret Book, 1993), 157.

Elder Gene R. Cook once recounted a conversation he had with rock superstar Mick Jagger. During the conversation, Jagger admitted. "Our music is calculated to drive the kids to sex." Elder Cook remembered: "He [Mick Jagger] told me the importance, in his view, of freeing up the youth. He felt that they ought to be able to do whatever they wanted in spite of their parents. He said that parents were inhibiting them too much and controlling things and they ought not to be doing that. It was truly astounding to me. He told me that he was thankful the family, as an entity, was being destroyed. And I gathered from what he was saying that *he was doing his best to help that along*."

This story only confirmed what I had already been feeling. The lyrics were powerful, yes. But the more subtle foe, the enemy more dangerous because it had not been fully recognized, was the corruption of the music itself. I believe that every feeling, every emotion that can be felt by man, can be expressed through music. This is true for every good and righteous emotion, but it is equally true for every sinful emotion and feeling. Music is not amoral any more than language is amoral. Music is the language of the heart. I began to see, to some degree, the true power of music. It can raise one to the highest heaven or sink one to the lowest hell.

How do we share emotion? How do we describe the affections of the heart? The most effective medium we have is music. Poetry is a mix of the mind and the heart, the blending of rhythm with words. The majority of our songs are a blend of poetic language with music. In other words, it is a blend of the heart and the mind. Music, however, is solely the language of the heart.

It is often argued that music is amoral. "All music is good! It is a matter of your individual taste or preference. It varies by personality." Common sense dictates otherwise, and the words of our inspired prophets agree. Ezra Taft Benson re-stated the following in October 1971:

 A letter from a concerned father about the evil effects of some popular music is one of many. I quote from this well-informed teacher of youth: 'Music creates atmosphere.

Atmosphere creates environment. Environment influences behavior. What are the mechanics of this process?

Rhythm is the most physical element in music. It is the only element in music that can exist in bodily movement without benefit of sound. A mind dulled by drugs or alcohol can still respond to the beat.

Loudness adds to muddling the mind. Sound magnified to the threshold of pain is of such physical violence as to block the higher processes of thought and reason. (And turning down the volume of this destructive music does not remove the other evils.) . . .

Repetition to the extreme is another primitive rock device. . . .

Gyrations, a twin to rock rhythm, are such that even clean hands and a pure heart cannot misinterpret their insinuations . . .

Darkness [and dimmed lights] is another facet of the rock scene. It is a black mass that deadens the conscience in a mask of anonymity. Identity lost in darkness shrinks from the normal feelings of responsibility.

Strobe lights split the darkness in blinding shafts that reduce resistance like the lights of an interrogator's third degree or the swinging pendulum of the hypnotist who would control your behavior. . . .

The whole psychedelic design [this father continues] is a swinging door to drugs, sex, rebellion, and Godlessness. Combined with the screaming obscenities of the lyrics, this mesmerizing music has borne the fruit of filth. Leaders of the rock society readily proclaim their degeneracy.

And the most diabolical deceit of this infamy is that it denies evil to be an absolute. Our religion is one of absolutes and cannot be rationalized into a relativistic philosophy of the 'liberal Mormons.' We cannot safely rationalize away righteousness.

What could be more misguided than fear that 'if rock music were not endorsed by our leaders, we may lose many young people.' (MIA music committee.) [Note that Elder Benson here corrects or chastises the leaders of one of the general auxiliaries of the Church] Even now we are losing them to the songs of Satan, drugs, sex, riot, and apostasy. We could be well reminded by a message from the Mormon Miracle pageant: 'Moroni knew that you cannot compromise with evil. If you do, evil always wins.' (Richard Nibley, excerpts from letter.) . . .

And now a music scholar points to 'a new direction in the rock-drug culture [which is] hailed by many ministers and the music industry as a silver lining in the clouds of gold. Religious rock is climbing up the 'Top Ten' charts. The growing resistance to the rock-drug scene is being diverted by this wholesome-appearing retreat from the new morality. But a review of religious rock materials unmasks an insidiously disguised anti-Christ. By reducing revealed religion to mythology, rock assumes the mantle of righteousness while rejecting the reality of sin. Without sin the new morality can continue in its Godless revel behind the pretense of religious robes. By reversing the roles of Jesus and Judas, one fast-selling album fits perfectly the warning of Isaiah [Isa. 5:20]: 'Woe unto them that call evil good, and good evil; that put darkness for light, and light for darkness.' (Richard Nibley.)[13]

Why then do we find music that clearly violates the instruction of the leadership of the Church permeating nearly every part of our current Church activities and programs? Many have

---

13   Ezra Taft Benson, "Satan's Thrust – Youth," *Ensign*, December 1971.

asked this question and been troubled by the irony. Thankfully, President Ezra Taft Benson, who I am sure struggled with this issue himself, gave this timeless counsel:

 Sometimes, from behind the pulpit, in our classrooms, in our council meetings, and in our Church publications, we hear, read, or witness things that do not square with the truth. . . . Now, do not let this serve as an excuse for your own wrongdoing. The Lord is letting the wheat and the tares mature before He fully purges the Church. He is also testing you to see if you will be misled. The devil is trying to deceive the very elect. Let me give you a crucial key to help you avoid being deceived. It is this-learn to keep your eye on the prophet. He is the Lord's mouthpiece and the only man who can speak for the Lord today. Let his inspired counsel take precedence. Let his inspired words be a basis for evaluating the counsel of all lesser authorities. Then live close to the Spirit so you may know the truth of all things.[14]

The words of our inspired prophets are clear. Music is *not* amoral. There is good music and there is bad music. Many of the musical elements we have come to accept and embrace, such as the off beat (otherwise known as the back beat or rock beat), repetition, gyrations, loudness, etc. are destructive. These compromises are a leading cause in the loss of a chosen generation of youth. Why? Music is the language of the heart with an ability to communicate *every* emotion of which we are capable.

---

14   Ezra Taft Benson, *Teachings of Ezra Taft Benson* (Bookcraft, 1988), 134; Ezra Taft Benson, *An Enemy Hath Done This* (Parliament Publishers, 1969), 317.

CHAPTER
Twelve

OUR PHILOSOPHY ON MOVIES

"The family is the simplest and smallest unit of society and the real fountain of culture. If this fountain remains pure, man's culture has promise. But if it becomes polluted, all the rest will turn to dust and ashes, since the home is the foundation of the entire social structure."

— Henry R. Van Til

Originally published by James F. Stoddard III on the Joseph Smith Foundation website. Reprinted here with minor edits.

Often when entertainment, specifically movies, are discussed in a Christian setting several phrases are used to justify compromising standards in what we chose to watch. Here are a few of the popular arguments:

"There is nothing bad in it!"

The issue is not whether there is anything bad in it, but rather whether there is anything good in it. The words "it is not enough to be good, we must be good for something" come to mind. "If there is anything virtuous, lovely, or of good report or praiseworthy, we [should] seek after these things." (Articles of Faith #13)

Mary & Ezra arm wrestling over which movie to watch—
Sense & Sensibility or Come What May

"It is rated PG, not R"

Do we really want those that set the ratings for movies to be our conscience? "For behold . . . it is given unto you to judge, that ye may know good from evil; and the way to judge is as plain, that ye may know with a perfect knowledge, as the daylight is from the dark night."(Moroni 7:15) In 1930 there was a very different rating system for movies. It was called the Motion Picture Production Code of 1930. It's moral standard would be considered today far better than "family entertainment." Think how far we have fallen. But think again. This code is at best Terrestrial—what would the Celestial code be?

"There were no sex scenes"

What about suggestive material? Crudeness? More importantly, what are the subtle dangers? How are marriage and families portrayed? Are large families promoted or ridiculed? Are Christian virtues shown to be the one true path to happiness, or are they looked upon as out of date or even mocked? Are breaking the law and living a carefree life glamorized? Is the purpose of life to become more like God, or is having fun, obtaining wealth, or just doing what you want held up as the final end?

"There was only one bad part in it"

"For behold, a bitter fountain cannot bring forth good water; neither can a good fountain bring forth bitter water; wherefore, a man being a servant of the devil cannot follow Christ; and if he follow Christ he cannot be a servant of the devil."(Moroni 7:11) Those that produce movies promote the values that they themselves possess. If a person's character is weak enough to put a "bad" scene in a movie, the entire movie will also contain the fruits of that producer's character.

Instead, we believe in watching movies that . . .

. . . *portray heroes as individuals who are honest.* Integrity is upheld as essential to a successful life. Characters who are dishonest will always be villains. Acts of dishonesty will always have undesired consequences. Additionally, good is portrayed as good and evil is portrayed as evil.

. . . *show the wisdom of being true and the folly of being false.* Disloyal characters are always antiheroes; heroes can always be depended upon. A life of integrity is shown as paying off in the end; all good deeds are portrayed as eventually being rewarded. Wickedness is always shown to eventually cause difficulty and sadness.

. . . *portray the breaking of the law of chastity as being evil and causing heartache, sorrow, depression and bitter consequences.* This is the sin next to murder (Alma 39:5), and heroic characters will sacrifice their lives before allowing their virtue to be taken.

. . . show men and women sacrificing for others in service and practicing great and simple deeds of benevolence. Happiness is shown being found in losing one's life serving God, family and country. Greediness is shown as creating misery and leading to regret. Heroes are shown building humanity and doing good to all around them.

. . . portray all of the noble virtues that can be found in mankind, and more importantly the ingredients in the character of God. Good characters are shown striving to change and become better with all their heart, might, mind and strength.

We especially value movies that . . .

. . . have heroes who believe in and follow the teachings of our beloved Master Jesus Christ. These heroes perform righteous works through faith and diligence. They have the hope of receiving the commendation from our Father, "Well done thou good and faithful servant." We enjoy movies that show men and women of faith enduring persecution, trial, and great adversity and finally triumph. We are extremely careful that sacred things are portrayed as sacred. Righteous and sacred works are never ridiculed or made fun of. Christian principles including principles of freedom are not degraded. Our Latter-day Saint hymns and primary songs are never rewritten in irreverent ways with loud music and tempos that have been forbidden by prophets of God.

Finally, we seek diligently through great effort to find movies which . . .

. . . uphold the family standards found in the Proclamation to the World on the family; including men and women remaining worthy through their lives and staying true to their marital vows and covenants. We refuse to allow into our homes anything that is not lovely, dignified, and pure. These movies contain beautiful and inspiring music and promote behavior of good report. The movies we watch add glory to our Father in Heaven and are worthy of His praise. His Holy Spirit can permeate our home because of the entertainment we prayerfully choose.

CHAPTER
Thirteen

RAISING THE BAR

". . . I give unto you to be the light of this people. A city that is set on a hill cannot be hid. Behold, do men light a candle and put it under a bushel? Nay, but on a candlestick, and it giveth light to all that are in the house; Therefore let your light so shine before this people, that they may see your good works and glorify your Father who is in heaven."

— 3 Nephi 12:14-16

When Dad was in his teenage years, he attended a fireside where Elder Hartman Rector Jr. made a comment that hit Dad straight at his core. He remarked that throughout the world, everyone was worried about being *too* good. "But," he said, "when you get older and look back at your life, you are *never* going to regret having lived the highest standard you could. You will never say to yourself, 'I wish I hadn't been so careful in my media selection,' or 'I wish I hadn't been so kind and charitable to my neighbors.' You will always look back and wish you had been *better*. Always live the best you can so you can live a life without regrets." Dad knew personally the ridicule for being "too good"—sometimes external pressure had led him to compromise, leaving him with bitter regrets. Later in life, he would often sit for hours

Meet online friends and share ideas for higher standards!

pondering, "*How do we create an environment where no one has to feel alone, abandoned, or afraid to be good?*"

You Are Not Alone

Dad was always thinking about "focusing out." It wasn't enough to study better dance. If we learned it for our home, we had to share it with others. If we found good recipes, we needed to share them with other families. Good music? Post your YouTube playlists publicly so others can find them. Did you watch a good movie? Share it on social media or post a review online. Everything was about sharing light—putting it high on a candlestick—and making every moment a missionary opportunity to spread the Gospel.

As we met and talked with many families during firesides and presentations, we began to recognize a common theme. Our family was not the only one feeling drawn to live higher standards—there were so many others! But, much as we had sometimes felt, they too felt isolated in their feelings and beliefs. Though it didn't look exactly the same for any two families, we began to recognize the need for a coordinated group where people could network and strengthen one another in their personal journey to pursue a fresh, new culture of refinement and nobility. In 2018, Dad decided it was time to make his long-held dream a reality. Thus, Raising the Bar was born.

Dad always loved to quote President Joseph F. Smith who taught that instead of "tearing down" the "houses" (meaning the lifestyles, beliefs, and practices) of our neighbors, we should instead build a "better house":

 We have no need to tear down the houses of other people (using this expression as a symbol). We are perfectly willing that they should live in the homes they have erected for themselves, and we will try to show them a better way. While we will not condemn that which they love and cherish above all other things in the world, we will endeavor to show them a better way and build them a better house, and then invite them kindly, in the spirit of Christ, of true Christianity, to enter the better dwelling. This is the principle, and I wish to impress it upon you this morning.[1]

The vision behind Raising the Bar is creating a place where Latter-day Saints are permitted to "build that better house" both by sharing how they are "raising the bar" and being inspired by the example of others. This can be done through social media posts, blog articles, in-person events, webinars, and so forth. Raising the Bar is an ideal where no one is criticized for raising their personal or family standards.

When our family lived in California, we were friends with members of the Pentecostal faith. Our friends did not feel comfortable with dancing of any kind—not the square dance, not the Virginia reel, not English country dance . . . nothing. Our family, on the other hand, had a very different standard. In fact, Dad loved to dance and our family believes it is an art that can and must be redeemed as part of the Restoration! In spite of our differences, however, we found common ground with our Pentecostal friends because we were both seeking to raise the bar. Each of us had chosen a higher standard because we knew the Lord was not comfortable with the worldly, lustful, degenerate,

1 Joseph F. Smith, *Gospel Doctrine* (Salt Lake City: Deseret Book Company, 1975), 256.

inappropriate dance infiltrating our culture. Instead of severing our friendship because we saw dance differently, we respected and learned from one another because we shared the same *goal*.

Sadly, our culture today is extremely negative, argumentative, and arrogant. Anyone who has participated in a slightly controversial discussion on Facebook knows that it can quickly turn ugly. Everyone who is striving to live higher standards has experienced mockery, belittlement, or ridicule. After being humiliated, scorned and hurt, many of the best people we know have left these circumstances scarred and afraid to speak. It hurts to stand out—to be 'different.' Dad remembered the bullying he had experienced in his younger years for being 'good,' and how he had succumbed to the temptation to hide his light in a way that didn't draw attention. Many of the best people we know are terrified to lift up their "light on a candlestick"; they are afraid to share who they are and what they believe. Dad felt *strongly* that this must change. He knew that it was a solemn duty of every believer to draw others to Christ, and the most powerful way to do that was to live higher standards, unapologetically, so that people could see the fruits of living the Gospel.

Raising the Bar is a place where, ideally, everyone will feel safe to live according to the dictates of their conscience without fear. The common ground behind all Raising the Bar members should be that we believe in being "better" and are striving to "raise the bar." Each person is at a different level and application can sometimes look different depending on the circumstance. However, by each building a "better house" and learning from others, we can all come closer to understanding and living Zion principles.[2]

Standards: A Secret Weapon For Our Children

Dad would often say, "God works with humble, honest and chosen people." Perhaps the single most effective—yet most underrated and neglected principle in helping children become converted to the Gospel and building a peaceful and united home—is implementing

2   Learn more about Raising the Bar at https://josephsmithfoundation. org/raisingthebar/.

Dad dancing the Virginia Reel with Eliza

higher standards in your family lifestyle. Each family has a culture: a way of living with attitudes, music, art, conversation, diet, and so forth. What does your family culture reflect about your beliefs and ideals? Two wise women once wrote:

 Pretend you could wipe the current cultural scene clean of all the filth, and redesign the whole thing—art, music, fashion, film, the works—to be what you think culture should be like. What would that be? This is exactly what your home, your wardrobe, and your iPod are—your own little tailor-made corners of culture. So what kind of aesthetics are you promoting? . . . If culture is religion externalized (Henry Van Til), that means these choices are not religiously neutral, and it's time for Christian women, the creators of home culture, to start knowing the difference. Even if the biggest stand you ever take for Christian culture is the music you play around the house, the art you hang on the wall, and the way you dress your children . . . that will make a difference.[3]

---

3   Anna Sofia and Elizabeth Botkin, "The Top 10 Things Girls Should Study (But Rarely Do)," BotkinSisters.com, August 21, 2013, https://

If we could give one plea to families throughout the Church, if we could pass on what, for us, has been the secret to bringing our family together—opening the door for an outpouring of revelation, and initiating incredible miracles allowing us to produce the content and work done by the Joseph Smith Foundation—this would be our message: your children need a cause. They need a battle to fight within an environment of cleanliness and purity so their channel of revelation will be direct and free from obstruction.

If you listen to heavenly music, you will have heavenly thoughts. If your children are listening to music of lust and rebellion, they will have lustful and rebellious thoughts. If you want your children to be humble, obedient, and open to the spirit, give them movies, music, food, and recreation that will bring that spirit into their lives. A home can be transformed simply by changing the standards.

Raise your posterity to lay down their lives for others. A generation raised on this foundation will be a generation who will build Zion. We are not waiting on the Lord—the Lord and the hosts of Heaven are awaiting *our* moment of decision. Will we answer the call and rise up as sons and daughters of Zion?

botkinsisters.com/article/the-top-10-things-girls-should-study-but-rarely-do.

CHAPTER
Fourteen

A MIGHTY CHANGE OF HEART

LEAH'S CONVERSION

*". . . what shall I do that I may be born of God, having
this wicked spirit rooted out of my breast, and receive
his Spirit . . . I will give up all that I possess . . . that I
may receive this great joy. . . . I will give away
all my sins to know thee . . ."*

— Alma 22:15, 18

*This chapter is written by Leah regarding her experience
gaining a testimony and witness for herself.*

One summer night, many years ago, I made a life-
changing decision that would shape who I am today.
I learned that if we want to participate in building the
Lord's Kingdom, we have to be perfectly obedient and cleanse
out anything in our lives that may be holding us back.

As I went through my early teens, I struggled with "catching
the vision," as Dad would put it. I could see the useful things
we were learning and creating, but my heart was not converted.
I woke up early, participated in 'the cause,' completed chores,
helped the younger kids with school and more, but rarely
felt driven to study the Gospel and build the Kingdom in my

spare time. The books, movies, and music that our ward and neighborhood were reading, watching, and listening to—such as *Marvel* movies, *Batman*, and *Hunger Games* seemed more exciting than what I had been taught was good. I began secretly watching them. Popular films brazenly showed immodesty, sexual innuendo, swearing, violence, lying, and magic. Morality and innocence were mocked, while a love for carnal things was fostered. Even more subtle were the philosophies of men mingled with scripture. Fathers were demeaned. Teenage rebellion was glorified. Music with an offbeat, which had been discouraged by Presidents of the Church, was used. And much more. I didn't like the inappropriate content, but I was entranced by the rest.

We had a high standard for movies in our home. Dad did not approve of Hollywood entertainment. I am extremely grateful now for the standard he set. Dad had studied scripture and prophetic teachings from a very young age. Latter-day prophets had warned against the corrupt influence of popular media which was being accepted by members of the Church. Dad had collected many quotes and scriptures teaching how to discern the agendas infused into our culture. Dad's research has changed the lives of many families. Dad often reminded us that our world was the most wicked of all earths.[1] He also taught us that Satan didn't care if we read our scriptures, only if we *applied* them.

My rebellious attitude during that time brought a detrimental spirit and attitude into my life and our home. My entertainment choices affected my time, spiritual sensitivity, and ability to receive inspiration. They also influenced my ability to do productive work on the animations and graphics for our videos. It was also hard to remember instructions and keep a patient, loving feeling in the house. On the outside, however, I knew every answer in Sunday School and appeared to be a model child.

There were times when I felt convicted by my conscience and threw all the 'junk' away—such as after a scripture discussion,

---

1   Moses 7:36.

watching a movie that depicted Christian persecution, or something that showed the consequences of our modern culture. But the 'junk' eventually came back. My heart still wanted it. I was looking for the next 'high,' if you will. I was empty and selfish—though I didn't realize it—looking for something to excite and interest me. I remember thinking at the time, and have thought since then, that sin is like a lot of little threads that bind you. You can clip those threads, but if you leave even one, it is a strong cord that binds you while the others are growing back.

Faced with a Choice

One July day when I was 17, I went on a walk with my Dad. He had discovered some of the books and movies I had been hiding. Very patiently, but also sadly and with pleading in his voice, Dad asked, "Is there any part of you that wants this other way?" He was asking if there was any part of me that was willing to give up what I *knew* was wrong. He asked if I cared about God's standard—if I wanted to *become like* God, not just *know* about Him. He was giving me a chance to open up, confess, and change. In spite of a thousand tiny voices inside of me, screaming that I couldn't, I decided to take the plunge. What started then was a journey that has led me to where I am today.

Dad asked what changed people, and guessing, I said, "Prayer?" He said no. Everything was silent as I racked my mind, trying to remember the answer. Up to this point, the Gospel had been mainly intellectual for me—a collection of memorized facts.

After a few minutes, Dad finally gave me the answer: "Sacrifice. *Sacrifice changes people.*"

I realized then that to be a true Christian I had to give up my *natural man* and not simply follow a few rules. I had to follow what God wanted me to do, at all times, in all things, and in all places. Dad explained that this was the purpose behind the baptismal covenant. Taking Christ's name upon me meant I would always act as He would act.

⌒

True conversion—a mighty change of heart—can only
come through sacrifice and obedience.

⌒

The Doctrine and Covenants states that, "By this ye may know if a man repenteth of his sins—behold, he will confess them and forsake them,"[2] so I decided to put this into practice. I thought through past mistakes, then confessed in detail to family members. I wanted to be honest, without holding anything back. It took me several hours to remember until I could think of nothing else. When I had finished, I felt that I had truly opened up the gate and started on the journey towards the Kingdom. I felt very humbled, but I had yet to truly feel the Godly sorrow that leads to repentance or experience a mighty change of heart.

After I got home, the process of cleaning out the trash began. I decided to set scriptural teachings as my only standard for what I believed and for how I acted. I realized that if I didn't compare my actions to scripture, which defines who/what "God" even is, then what other standard could I have? Doctrine truly changes behavior. I deleted corrupt books off of the Kindle. I went through my Pinterest boards and removed anything that would tempt me to go back or that would pull me away from God. I threw away physical reminders of book series or movies that might be distracting. I also cleaned out my music playlists, and replaced unworthy songs with uplifting, inspiring music. These may appear to be trivial or inconsequential things, but I knew what my heart was most attached to and what burdened my conscience.

That night when I said my prayers, they felt real and sincere for the first time in a long while. When I was young, I had felt closer to God and had experienced many miraculous events— but as I grew older, I had drifted. I felt as though I didn't know enough about the God I had prayed to. I knew a lot of head knowledge, facts, and numbers. I could recite Church history

---

2   Doctrine & Covenants 58:42-43.

stories and rattle off a bunch of Gospel trivia I had learned, but I didn't know *who* God was.

I also felt conflicted because even though I had confessed my sins, deleted and thrown away my books and movies, I knew that going forward, I needed to make an eternal commitment. I was still sitting on the fence and had not yet drawn a permanent line in the sand. I knew from spiritual experiences earlier in my life that the power of the devil is very strong. Part of my heart still wanted the trash I had cleaned out, and that desire, if unrestrained, would grow stronger. I didn't want to be neutral, but instead, pick one side or the other—either commit my life to Christ and follow Him in every word and deed, or follow Satan. Both had power, and I would fight for one side or the other. I didn't want to wait even one more day, because with each passing moment, it seemed impossible to be 'neutral.' It seemed like a huge decision—a decision that would affect what I chose to eat, how I talked, how I walked, how I sat, what I said, what skills I would pursue, my thoughts—everything.

As I was pondering which path to take, I remembered my Dad had often talked about our ancestry. My sixth great-grandfather was also the grandfather of Joseph Smith. Many Latter-day prophets and apostles had taught that Joseph Smith was a descendant of Jesus Christ.[3] I thought to myself, *"If I actually have the blood of Christ running through me right now, how can I choose to oppose Him? How can I deny my own blood—the same blood that flows in me? That would be like saying red is black. I can't be a Judas and turn traitor."* Understanding my bloodline set the final weight on my decision. I decided I would follow Christ. Since then, understanding my heritage and ancestry has influenced many of my decisions.

Replacing Evil with Good

The next few days felt very hollow. Clean and pure, but hollow, like *things* were missing. I had to replace pleasure with better,

---

3 Please see the documentary, *Hidden Bloodlines: The Grail & the Lost Tribes in the Lands of the North* (DVD).

holier pursuits and activities. Over the next month or two, and even the next few years, I tried to discover what true, lasting joy is, and how it can be experienced and described. Through obedience, I learned to change the desires of my heart.

⟋⟍

When raising standards, we cannot only cut entertainment which desensitizes our spirit—we must replace the empty void with good and fill our lives with pure media, music, and recreation.

⟋⟍

At first, I knew the movies and culture I had embraced in the past were bad, but I was emotionally blind to many of the faults I didn't want to see. I did not hate sin. I realized I had this weakness and started comparing characters and scenes to scripture and noble examples to find out what was right and wrong.

Sacrifice brings forth the blessings of heaven—both for those who give and those who receive. I started reading many inspiring books and watching movies about persecuted Christians who had given everything for Christ. I looked forward to receiving our monthly copy of a free magazine called *The Voice of the Martyrs*. I devoured *God's Double Agent* in only two days! This brought an incredible spirit into my life. I wanted to create a website called "Refiner's Fire"[4] where people could find stories and examples of conversion from both scripture and other

---

4 If you would like to learn more, or share your own conversion story, visit https://hereistandnow.com/stoddard/refinersfire.

sources. I even designed a logo while we were driving home from working on our farm.

Now, besides my scriptures, my favorite books and movies are about Christian missionaries and martyrs. Their stories and examples inspire me and many other people. Many of the movies, documentaries, and books I started to read and watch are included in the following list:

Books

- *The Heavenly Man* by Brother Yun
- *God's Smuggler* by Andrew van der Bijl
- *Tortured for Christ* by Richard Wurmbrand
- *Words of Joseph Smith*, a collection of Nauvoo discourses by Joseph Smith
- *The Pastor's Wife* by Sabina Wurmbrand
- *I Found God In Soviet Russia* by John H. Noble
- *These Are The Generations* by Eric Foley
- *Hearts of Fire* by The Voice of the Martyrs
- *Into the Den of Infidels*, a collection of Muslim conversion stories by Voice of the Martyrs
- *Captive in Iran* by Maryam Rostampour and Marziyeh Amirizadeh, and their experience in Evin Prison
- *Seeking Allah, Finding Jesus* by Nabeel Qureshi
- *The Hiding Place* by Corrie Ten Boom
- *I Dared to Call Him Father* by Bilquis Sheikh
- *Restricted Nations* series by The Voice of the Martyrs
- *Tortured for His Faith* by Haralan Popov
- *I Will Die Free* by Humberto Noble Alexander
- *The Persecutor* by Sergei Kourdakov
- *God's Double Agent* by Bob Fu
- *Vanya: A True Story* by Myrna Grant
- *The Voice of the Martyrs* (Magazine)

Movies & Documentaries

- *China Cry* (1990)
- *For Greater Glory* (2012)

- *On Wings of Eagles* (2016)
- *The Printing* (1990)
- *Tortured for Christ* (2018)
- *Sabina: Tortured for Christ - The Nazi Years* (2022)
- *Bamboo in the Winter* (1991)
- *The Least of These* (2019)
- *Polycarp* (2015)
- *Bless You, Prison* (2002)
- *Behind the Sun* (1995)
- *Gold Through the Fire* (1987)
- *Flame in the Wind* (1971)
- *God's Outlaw* (1986)
- *The Radicals* (1989)

- *Sarah's Trail of Blood* (2007)
- *Free Burma Rangers* (2020)
- *The Insanity of God* (2016)
- *Messenger of the Truth* (2013)

Discovering a New Hunger for the Scriptures

As time passed, I realized I was hungry to learn more about the God I had committed my life to. I started delving into the scriptures—not from obligation or conformity, but because I wanted to understand the purpose of life and how God wanted me to live. Dad's life had blessed many people because he knew the scriptures very well, and I also desired to do the same.

~

"Those who have read [the scriptures], and who have drunk of the stream of knowledge which they convey, know how to appreciate them."[5] — *Joseph Smith*

~

---

5   Joseph Smith, Letter to Saints Scattered Abroad, September 1840, p. 179, Joseph Smith Papers.

Ezra followed Leah's example—delving into a family favorite biography of Andrew van der Bijl, who secretly smuggled Bibles behind the Iron Curtain

The scriptures became my comfort and standard, so I started memorizing long passages, which I could then recite to myself during hard days working on our family farm or during family struggles. Alma 5 and 7:14-15, Mormon 9:25-29, 1 John 3:13-22, and 1 Nephi 15:24, especially stood out to me. I began fasting every week. I also started spending more time working with and listening to my Dad, who patiently guided and loved me. We went on walks together, no matter the time of year—rain or shine, sometimes even in freezing temperatures. We'd freely talk and express opinions about what I had accomplished, what I was learning in my scriptures, house management, and other subjects—no matter how 'radical.' We would discuss questions such as:

- What is the difference between 'grace to grace' and 'grace for grace'? (Doctrine & Covenants 93)

- How can Christ atone for our sins when we can't atone for another person's sins?

- How does the Atonement actually work?

- What does Lehi mean when he says redemption can only come 'in and through' the Messiah? Why does he use the word 'in' and what does that mean? How can redemption be 'in' Him?

Around this time, we started researching the possibility that some Nephites had migrated to other countries, and the scriptural evidence behind this theory. I started collecting documents full of scripture references, questions, and key points regarding this theory. I read through the Book of Mormon with new eyes and pondered on every verse. It has since become my favorite book of all! In the Book of Mormon, we see that the central key is true conversion and missionary work. My Dad suggested that I read the book *Words of Joseph Smith*, and as I read it, my mind was opened. I had never before experienced such clarity, wisdom, and power. It was by reading this book years ago that I obtained a testimony of Joseph Smith as a prophet of God. I realized that if other people read Joseph Smith's words they could also obtain the same insights and testimony. We started sorting his quotes by topic with a plan to publish an organized topical 'Joseph Smith Teachings' book.

I started listening to audiobooks and talks by Joseph Fielding Smith and Ezra Taft Benson, especially "A Mighty Change of Heart" and "Born of God." I'd read both of these before, but they took on a new meaning for me as I *lived* the teachings. My conversion did not happen when I made the decision to follow Christ, but instead as I *obeyed* every principle I knew, my desires slowly changed.[6] Our obedience and receiving a new heart from the Lord are the keys to our conversion, and we cannot fake it. Ezra Taft Benson said it perfectly when he stated:

---

6   Mosiah 5:1-5; Alma 19:33.

> The Lord works from the inside out. The world works from the outside in. The world would take people out of the slums. Christ takes the slums out of people, and then they take themselves out of the slums. . . . Christ changes men, and changed men can change the world. Men changed for Christ will be captained by Christ. Like Paul they will be asking, "Lord, what wilt thou have me to do?" Peter stated they will "follow his steps." John said they will "walk, even as he walked."[7]

I experienced another turning point in my life when we started working on the video, *Hidden Bloodlines: The Grail & the Lost Tribes in the Lands of the North*. Whenever the story of Christ visiting England or His descendants came up, I felt such a powerful spirit, more than any other scriptural topic. This subject, along with the song "Jerusalem" by William Blake, opened my eyes even more to my heritage. Of all the projects our family has worked on, this was by far my favorite. If others knew their birthright, how would it affect their decisions?

Won Through Patient Love

Everything did not change overnight, however. So much of our modern culture—the attitudes, rebellion, arrogance, pessimism—was still embedded inside me. So much trash had accumulated over the years. Temptation to return to the flashy, attractive movies, and sometimes books, pulled at me many times. Sometimes I started slipping back, but if I know one thing, it is that God will truly bend over backwards to help you change. My Dad was also a perfect example of this, and he never gave up on me—often spending hours late at night talking me through concerns, even when he had to go to work early in the morning and also struggled with severe insomnia. He never complained *once* about taking time to talk with me. I always thank God that my Dad never gave up on me or stopped trying to convert me.

---

7   Ezra Taft Benson, "Born of God," *Ensign*, July 1989.

A few years after I cleaned out my culture, my Dad told me that the movies I had watched would affect me negatively for many years to come. At the time, I considered this a challenging statement to swallow as I had worked very hard to create a clean culture and weed out ideologies that affected my character. However, over the years, I have remembered his comment and found it is *very true*! These films affect not only our thoughts, but our attitudes, perspective on authority, sensitivity to sin, and more. I am grateful that Dad was honest with me. The impact of what I had watched and read weighed heavily on my mind, as well as the time I had wasted in frivolous pursuits, causing me much pain and tears of regret. How many people had not been helped because I had spent my time just "having fun"? I had been blessed with knowledge that could change the lives of many families, but what had I done with it? Would some of my siblings struggle because of my bad example? Had I placed an extra burden on my family? While Dad worked tirelessly at a software job making money for his family and the cause, what had I been doing? I lacked spiritual insights and felt blocked from the presence of God.

There were many times when I cried myself to sleep as I realized the consequences of my actions, for myself and others. I was afraid that the blessings given to me as a child would no longer be mine. Slowly, I learned to trust God, and have since then experienced many miracles, moments of inspiration, blessings, and also a remission of my sins. I have been redeemed. My Dad would often recite this quote from the Prophet Joseph Smith:

 Our heavenly father is more liberal in his views, and boundless in his mercies and blessings, than we are ready to believe or receive, and at the same time is more terrible to the workers of iniquity, more awful in the executions of his punishments, and more ready to detect every false *way* than we are apt to suppose him to be.[8]

---

8   Joseph Smith, Letter to Nancy Rigdon, circa Mid-April 1842, p. 2, The Joseph Smith Papers; emphasis in original.

Experiencing a Remission of My Sins

My tastes in music, movies, and books have changed extremely—an act of God's grace, for I could not have done it on my own. Before experiencing true joy, I didn't realize I had lived an unhappy, unfeeling life. I continue to study the battlelines[9] to learn what makes those books, movies and music so deceptive and alluring. Our culture is calculated and fashioned to prey on weaknesses in human nature—our "natural man." Satan knows that if he can destroy our morality, then our families, our government, our economy, and everything else will *fail*. The ways to sin are diverse,[10] and our world is full of them.

Our rebellious culture is strong, enticing, and ever-present. It's in our toys, food, stores, billboards, cars, stickers, movies, music, books, and more. I've talked with many parents who are wanting, or creating, a more holy environment in their homes. I've also talked with many youth who were in the same spot I was years ago—reading the same books and watching the same things—wondering if they should or shouldn't give them up. After pulling out media and entertainment which desensitizes and is "without feeling," we must fill the empty void with good, replacing the counterfeit with the true substance. We need to follow the Lord's example as closely as possible to avoid being deceived. As Charles Spurgeon said, "Discernment is not knowing the difference between right and wrong. It is knowing the difference between right and almost right."

At the end of the day, however, even the most pure environment cannot change our natural man. I firmly believe that each individual must come to a point, especially in our world today, where they decide whether or not they want to be a true Christian

---

9 Inspired by a Christian who did the same thing, my family put together a list of Gospel principles, along with their Satanic counterfeits. Under each "Battleline," for example, "Creationism & Children of God vs. Darwinism & the Descent of Man," you can find a list of resources to further your knowledge and study. Learn more at: https://josephsmithfoundation.org/battlelines.

10 Mosiah 4:29-30.

and seek the Lord in all they do and say. This cannot be done by force—only through love and persuasion. Rules can and should be applied, but they cannot forcefully change the *heart*. Each of us has been given the gift of *free will* which we will either increase or abuse. There is no formula for a change of heart, though the way to gain it is so simple: willing sacrifice, faith, and help from the Lord.

We have also found many other families who are striving to raise their own standards and create stronger family relationships. I have seen many other adults, youth, and even children receive a change of heart as they learn these principles. The difference in their personality is a testimony that God can change *any* of us.

If we have been blessed to know the answers to many of our society's problems, how can we not share them? What responsibilities lie on our shoulders? If we don't share the knowledge we've been given, it would be better to not have known.

Without my Dad's love, example, and persistent guidance, and inspiration and help from the Lord, I could not have been converted. Today, I am a different person than I was before. I can truly testify of having my own change of heart many times throughout my life, by learning and applying scriptural principles practically.

CHAPTER
Fifteen

HEALING & BEAUTY FROM ASHES

"Nearer my God to thee, nearer to thee
E'en though it be a cross that raiseth me."

— *Sarah F. Adams, "Nearer, My God, To Thee"*

This chapter is going to be a difficult one for us. The emotions associated with speaking publicly about vulnerable and traumatic experiences in your past is difficult to understand unless you have walked a similar road. It's a big step to make, but God uses trials in our lives to refine corrupt metal into gold. When we whitewash history—past or present—when we attempt to paint the life of a Christian as a smooth-sailing pleasure voyage, we lose touch with reality and what being a Christian really looks like. We fail to understand the true meaning of discipleship. No great man or woman lived without trial. In telling our story, we want to be upfront about the full picture. We want to bear testimony that God can help anyone get through the most difficult of situations, regardless of any choices made by others. If we are faithful to Him, He can create beauty from ashes.

Our Mom struggled mentally and emotionally throughout most of our childhood. She went through phases: there were highs, and there were lows. During her highs, she was an amazing

Mom. She was caring, involved, supportive, and one of the most hard-working women we knew. She loved the Gospel. During her lows, however, she became a different person. She would struggle with manipulation, dishonesty, and intense anger. During some of these dark phases, many of us children were physically and/or emotionally abused. This is not an exposé—nor is this a book centered on our complete history, or an extensive discussion on healing from abuse. We will merely share that we *have* experienced trauma, and so we speak from experience and authenticity when we testify that Jesus Christ's principles can help individuals overcome *any* hardship. The painful fact is that in the fallen world in which we live, most have experienced abuse in some form. If this includes you, know that you are not alone and there *is* hope and healing through Christ. Moreover, we know with surety that if we choose obedience to God, He can and will work mighty miracles on our behalf. Nothing can stop the work of the Lord from progressing. We know that becoming involved in the Lord's cause is the way to truly experience the healing power of Christ.

Healing From Abuse: Leah Stoddard

Sharing my story is one of the hardest things I have ever written in my life. As I write, the emotions tied to reliving painful memories and traumatic experiences from my past are overwhelming. I hope that someone can be helped by what I am about to share. Perhaps you may have gone through similar experiences yourself.

During my childhood, my Mom suffered with mood swings—extreme ups and downs. At times, she was the best Mom in the world, looking out for my needs and buying me things that made my life easier and more enjoyable. At other times, she struggled. I didn't know how to react or respond when she became angry and hurt me both physically and emotionally. I love my Mom and have no desire to injure her character or demean her, but rather share my experience of how I learned to forgive and overcome the effects of abuse through the Gospel, which has transformed and shaped my character. So often we turn to formulas, self-help books, and daily affirmations too quickly without realizing that the Gospel, a *free* gift from God, is the only thing that can truly heal a crushed soul. The Gospel of Jesus Christ is more than memorized facts and figures, but real power—something that works *permanently*.

As a child, I never considered the abuse was anyone's fault but mine. I did not understand why she called me, among many things, a "retard," a "bitch," or "dumb," nor did I understand what I had done to deserve these labels. These remarks crushed my confidence and shattered my feelings. As I grew older, I noticed that it seemed to give her satisfaction if I reacted to her abuse with emotion or pain (at least during her dark phases). It was better to appear passive and unaffected. While my Dad was at work, my sister Hannah did her best to create a peaceful and safe home. However, when they were both gone, a more chaotic and inconsistent environment reigned. I often walked on eggshells, but even then could not learn how to 'play the game' well enough to avoid Mom's explosions.

As I grew older, her explosive moments became increasingly physical and unpredictable, which resulted in bruises, scars, welts, excessive spanking with metal spoons on our backs, poking forks deep into my back over and over as to intentionally cause pain, withholding food, etc. She struggled with self-confessed anger, hate, jealousy, and dishonesty; but in her heart I know she wanted to be a good mother. At times she would be very kind, but during her dark moments, she made many hurtful and sarcastic comments, calling me "fat," a "witch," and "stupid;" she also told me I had "brain problems," a "victim mentality," that I should be "locked in a mental institution," that she didn't want me here, etc. At times, she lied and told siblings false statements and stories about other siblings in order to create distrust and fear among us. In her mind she wanted a house that was orderly, peaceful, smooth, and beautiful, but her dark times destroyed trust and prevented her from connecting with her children. Had I responded in a more consistent, forgiving, Christ-like manner, I think some conflicts could have been avoided.

During my teen years, running stairs became a form of punishment, most often for very minor issues or typical child accidents, or to vent when she was angry. I would frequently be required to run up and down 100+ times. As I climbed those wooden stairs, I swore with each step, up and down, up and down, over and over again, that I could *not* be crushed. I would win in the end. If I refused to run, I would be spanked and sent to run again. At this time, the strain on my knees was so severe that they would dislocate at random times in the day, even during my sleep, and I would cry out in agony when I couldn't push them back until they would slip back in on their own. This caused permanent damage as they are still weak, and to this day, I cannot kneel properly. She also had us get into a plank as a punishment or put our hands straight into the air for long periods of time. I responded with bitterness and resentment. In anger she told me that if I ever told anyone what had happened, the 'government' would come in, split our family up, and I would never see my siblings again. I was consumed with frustration, helplessness, and loathing. At other times, however, Mom was calm and helpful, and my anger died down, and I would forgive and forget—until the cycle repeated itself.

Abuse did not occur when my Dad or older sister were home. If any situation started to get tense, both of them would diffuse and handle the situation. They knew Mom could become very emotional, but they always stepped in so they never saw the lengths she would go to when there was no check. I did not bring up issues to either of them, because I knew the consequence of doing so would be even more severe for me when they left the next day. Dad trusted Mom too much and he couldn't fathom anything like this could really happen until it was too late. Years later, Dad cried when I finally found my voice and began sharing what had happened while he was gone.

Overcoming Survival Tendencies

Mom was not angry all the time though. There were many times when she was workable and solved issues patiently. She was also a very hard worker and generally listened when I was talking. She loved interior decorating and had a good sense of colors and style. She tried to be loving and helpful and wanted to know about her kids' thoughts and dreams. Her instability and unpredictable character was very confusing to me as I tried to navigate my life.

At one point I also succumbed to temptation to read or watch things that made it harder to feel the Spirit, which affected my judgment and attitude.[1] Abuse taught me to see life as a game, a place where the strong survived, but the weak were crushed. In my mind, if I wasn't strong or smart enough, I didn't make it. Sometimes this was true! Mom could abuse my body, I thought, but she couldn't touch my mind!

I had not surrendered my heart and life to Christ at this point, so when conflict arose, I often became bitter. Through trial and error, I learned to manipulate and to navigate the manipulation being done to me. I would avoid telling her what I liked and disliked—often telling her the opposite so she could not use it against me. I closed off my emotions and decided to avoid opening up and trusting others. I was afraid of being physically touched—I couldn't hug even my family and felt uncomfortable with perfectly normal physical contact. I watched other members of my family also become used and abused. When she was angry, I saw myself absorbing her misery and hate—and it scared me.

When I was about 17, however, I had a change of heart experience where I cleaned out media and books that were destroying me spiritually, and I began a new life. This brought a new perspective, and I started to see how much I had developed a "survival of the fittest" mentality, which deeply affected my decisions, treatment of family members, and mindset. As I worked to overcome the survival techniques I had adopted, I prayed to be given a new heart and perspective. Playing hymns like "Come, Come Ye Saints," "A Poor Wayfaring Man of Grief," and "Jesus, Once of Humble Birth," in addition to other hymns

---

1   To read Leah's full conversion story, see Chapter 14: A Mighty Change of Heart - Leah's Conversion.

and songs, helped me understand what the Spirit of the Lord feels like, and how the Lord lived His own life. The following are some of my thoughts as I have compared and contrasted the Gospel with a survival perspective.

Survival of the Fittest	*Jesus Christ/Gospel*
First priority is to protect and support yourself. Punish enemies and take vengeance into your own hands.	Forgive and do not pursue vengeance on your enemy—that is God's responsibility. Justice must be sought and firm protections should be put in place—but should be done in love and according to principle for both parties.
Strong survive while the weak die out.	Strongest lay down their life for the weak. The most fit of all (Jesus Christ) died for the unfit (you and me).
Strong prey on and use the weak to survive.	Strong build up the weak, even at their own expense. Both the strong and weak serve sacrificially to the best of their ability.
Driving emotion is fear.	Driving emotion is love.
Actions are driven by natural man instincts, appetite, and unrestrained urges.	Actions are guided by principles and laws from God in scripture. Inappropriate urges are restrained.
You are a victim of your environment and genetics.	Through Jesus Christ and obedience, any environment and genetic tendencies can be overcome.

You bear scars forever.	Complete healing is possible.
Human nature is controlled with external rules and force.	God softens our hearts and changes our very nature to become Christlike.

Eliminating Anger & Fighting

As the years passed, Mom's 'dark phases' seemed to increase. In an attempt to cope with her frustration, she abdicated a lot of parenting and homeschooling to Hannah and me. Unfortunately, she would also lie to my Dad about our character and household events, which often made life difficult and straining. Sometimes we just had to bite our tongue and prove our true character through time and fruits.

Verbal abuse seemed to explode with increasing regularity. One day, in my late teens, when she became physically abusive, I even ran away from home and hid by a neighbor's barn for hours, waiting for my Dad or Hannah to get home so it would be safe to return.

Dad always tried to limit fighting and contention in our home, but at this particular time he was suffering from some very serious health problems. He was almost forced to go to the emergency room following the loss of a lot of blood. We were all frustrated, and patience had worn thin—too thin. Mom began threatening divorce and using it to manipulate situations. One day, Mom got into an argument and yelled at me, Hannah, and Dad. This was an evening when both Hannah and Dad had not been feeling well—not to mention the fact that this was the culmination of many days of strife when Mom had been experiencing a serious down mood. Following her outburst at us, she excused herself from the room, and when she returned she acted uncharacteristically cool and collected. We were confused by the change in her attitude, but at this point we were very frustrated. We were distressed and annoyed and lost control, and we made comments we did not mean to say. This does not excuse us, but it was a result of frustration that finally came to a boiling point.

Dad felt really bad about the argument. A little later, he wrote a beautiful letter to Mom after several days without sleep:

 First off, this may not be very good, because I haven't slept for days, but I at least wanted to say something and maybe [I] can do a better job later. . . . I want to just say sorry that I have hurt your feelings by things that I have said. . . . I will do everything in my power, which hopefully means I will never talk in these frustrated and upset ways again. . . . I haven't been able to sleep for days because I wish I could have done better. I believe you know I try very hard to do the right thing, but I can now see that I must work so much harder to help you feel loved, respected and honored. Things got too crazy. . . . Just let us know what you want so that you can be happy and we will do all we can to make it happen. In thinking this over we just need to make sure I am far more careful in making sure you are feeling like your needs are being met and that you are being heard. . . . Sorry doesn't mean much, what you need is actions [on our part] so we will work to make that happen.

Dad had made plans to slow down, and emphasize family activities and councils to help. Mom agreed and appeared cheerful and positive, but a few days later, while we were recording narration for a video, Mom left with my younger siblings, telling them they were going to a park. When night came, they still hadn't returned. No one was answering her phone, and we became worried about their safety. Did they get into an accident? Did the car run out of gas? Were they okay? My Mom eventually called and said she was leaving us. We later learned this had been premeditated on her part. She wouldn't allow Hannah and me to see her or our siblings again for two weeks. The trauma and shock was so severe on Dad's health that he never fully recovered. The night she left, his body went into shock, and he lost feeling in his legs and abdomen. We debated whether or not to take him to the emergency room, but this episode passed.

Dad, Hannah, and I wanted to apologize for the fight with Mom. I was very hurt that she had walked out on our family after everything we had been through, but I did want to follow Jesus Christ, forgive, and resolve the contention and bad feelings. Still, Mom wouldn't even talk to me or Hannah. We tried to apologize for anything we had done wrong, and yet she had no desire to build a bridge of any kind. She came through our house and took many—mostly expensive—items, including my only blazer, which I had worn while filming our video, *Hidden Bloodlines*. She also stole hundreds of dollars worth of items from our property. Later, Mom told us she had recorded the fight, and she began circulating an abridged version of the conversation. I listened to the audio file in shock. It was skewed to be favorable to her, and she had eliminated parts where she didn't look good. She then lied about the backstory and the circumstances surrounding the recording, disguising the true nature of the conversation. I felt played, disgusted, and betrayed. Her lies were stirring up others to anger against myself, my family members—including my father and siblings— for those who didn't know us. She had even secretly read and photocopied some of our journals, later circulating them to people we didn't even know just to mock, taunt, and ridicule us.

At times I thought I had forgiven Mom, but one day, the subject of her abuse came up and hostile feelings poured out in my voice and attitude. Dad asked that we cut the conversation short until we could speak with love and forgiveness. We needed to work through things, but anger was not the solution.

My Mom continued to spread slander and false statements about the morality and character of Dad, my siblings, and me. Some have claimed that our concerns with Mom were because Dad stirred us up against her—'parental alienation.' This is *completely* false. On the contrary, too often growing up, Dad would side with Mom, overly trusting her honesty and mental stability. As children, we saw a different perspective—a perspective born from experience.

Dad would often sit on the couch and say, "We need to love everyone, and if we have hate in our hearts, the Spirit of the Lord can't be here." I would sometimes find myself making sarcastic comments now and then, but Dad would *not* allow them in his presence. He also made a rule that no fighting or arguing of any kind was allowed in our home from that point. At times when I would get testy while working with a sibling or even my Dad, he would calm the situation, and we would go on a walk and talk through the issue or another unrelated subject until my temper cooled down. Sometimes he was really firm because he wasn't going to compromise on this rule ever again.

I still struggled with forgiveness. It was one thing to forgive after an injury, but it was difficult when peppered with constant slander, jabbing, and defamation. However, there came a point when I knew that I couldn't continue being angry. It was impeding the progress of projects that the Lord needed done and inhibiting inspiration. I knelt by the side of my bed and *prayed hard* with everything in me for God to pull the hate and anger out of my heart. I felt I should stay on my knees until I knew I had nothing but love for Mom. It took some time, but gradually I felt the frustration leaving me as I understood that the person Mom had become was not really herself. God still loved her and wanted her to be happy to the best of her ability. I started to feel love enter my heart and also peace about the situation. I saw her later that day and felt impressed to approach and talk with her. I told her that I forgave her for her past abuse, a comment which she brushed aside tersely, but surprisingly, it did not shatter the peace in my heart. I didn't need her to stop fighting to forgive. It was between me and the Lord. I couldn't remove the feelings of bitterness on my own—and I had tried—but as I came to God with pure intent, a willingness to do right, and demonstrating faith, those feelings were taken *away*.

A few months after Dad passed, my heart was breaking because Mom had recently abused several of my siblings, both emotionally and physically. As I sat milking our dairy goats one wintry afternoon, I felt so helpless and paralyzed, struggling to comprehend and crying out to God, "*Where are you?*" The situation seemed impossible to fix—I could do nothing but wait. Later that day, the thought came to me that I should start playing the Book of Mormon on audio while I was milking and doing farm chores. Our dear friend, Julie, had recently hosted her annual online Book of Mormon read-a-thon for Christmas with friends and family, and she told me that it had brought a wonderful spirit of peace into their home. I started playing the Book of Mormon audiobook every morning and night as I milked our goats, and it brought an amazing spirit of peace. A few days later, I was milking again and suddenly noticed that I no longer felt any anger or hate toward Mom. My mind drifted to the abuse done to my siblings which before had made me so frustrated. I instead felt calm and peaceful. Even after listening to a video and audio recording of her inflicting abuse on my siblings, I still didn't feel hate. I started to recall all the instances where people in the scriptures learned to forgive: Nephi, the Anti-Nephi-Lehies, Alma, Joseph of Egypt, Joseph Smith, the pioneers, and of course, Jesus. God has placed all of us here, and He has a plan. In the end, He will exchange beauty for ashes, and no damage can be so permanent that we cannot be changed. If God has forgiven us for everything we have done, how can we not forgive others?

I have a firm testimony that through prayer, fasting, and seeking to live more purely, the Lord can and will take away our anger and give us the spirit of forgiveness. Adding hate to more hate is not the answer—it is that same spirit of contention that drives *all* animosity and frustration. Only charity, which is the pure love of Christ, can overcome enmity. Sometimes we have to pray "with all the energy of heart"[2] for this kind of charity, but it can happen; it is real, and it does have *power*.

A Child's Prayer: Hannah Stoddard

Since I was young, I have seen Mom go through what I call "angry phases." She would become very hostile, vindictive, overwhelmed, emotional, and anxious. Her memory was especially weak during these times. She would often be in the middle of a conversation and forget what someone else said or

---

2 Moroni 7:48.

what her original point was. I have always loved and still love my Mom. When I was young, I would often feel hurt, angry and isolated when she would experience periods of anger. I didn't understand why she was acting differently. Sometimes, I blamed myself. However, when I was about fourteen or fifteen, I realized these were temporary episodes that would eventually pass. At first the fluctuation frightened me. I can remember being ten years old and having a feeling of confusion and even dread come over me as her voice seemed to change, her demeanor would change, her countenance would change, her reaction to everyday events would change. She would truly become a different person. Dad always taught us to be loyal and true to our family—that if someone was trying to change, we should love and support them in that process, not tear them down and expose them to ridicule. I remember consciously watching my Mom and trying to put this principle into practice. She needed help, not censure.

When I was 14, there was one day that had been particularly challenging. After everyone was fast asleep, I was still awake, buried underneath my blankets, crying and crying, and I felt as if I could never stop. This was unique for me because I had always prided myself on being strong and resilient. "*Stoddards don't cry,*" I would tell myself. I was a descendant of military generals and soldiers dating back thousands of years. You don't break, you stand firm . . . right?

But this time, my Mom was in one of her dark phases, and I was broken. Not only had the verbal abuse been intense, but I also felt betrayed. I was trying so hard to be good, but I didn't know what to do.

Tossing and turning, I struggled in vain to find anything to bring me solace. Finally, I listened to a quiet voice inside that prompted me to pray. In the darkness, I softly began singing to myself, "A Child's Prayer." I loved this song, but this time it took on new meaning—every word I murmured came straight from the heart. "*Heavenly Father, are you <u>really</u> there? And do you hear and answer every child's prayer?*"

Suddenly, the most profound feeling of peace, love, and forgiveness for Mom came over me. The ridicule and aggressive language that had been repeating over and over inside my head vanished and pure peace and charity came in their stead. While her actions were inappropriate, I could take the higher path, forgive, and do all I could as her daughter to help her. My tears were literally wiped away. I basked for a while in peace. "*God is not only real,*" I thought, "*but He actually is aware of me at this very moment.*" As I drifted off to sleep, I gave a prayer of thanks—but in a childlike moment of simple faith, for some reason appended the words: "*You know the only thing missing? A rainstorm. I certainly would love a rainstorm right now.*" I've always been a lover of rainstorms and thunder—those moments when it seems as if God Himself is speaking. The days surrounding this night had been hot and dry, not a cloud in the sky. But still, it was a passing wish, although an idle one.

When I woke up in the morning and opened my blinds, I was so dumbfounded that I can still vividly remember my shock over a decade later. It was raining outside! Beautiful raindrops were falling everywhere. I immediately began crying in my room. I struggled to comprehend what I was feeling. I always knew God performed 'big' miracles. He saved the Israelites by parting the Red Sea, He fed hungry multitudes with miraculously appearing loaves and fishes, He healed the sick and raised Lazarus from the dead—but giving a fourteen-year-old a rainstorm just because she liked it? I began to see God in a different light. He was not only the God of Abraham, Isaac, and Jacob, but He was also *my* God. Personally, it felt, God was tutoring me in an important lesson: that He will be there no matter what I experience. I believe any of us can be utterly alone—you can be powerless, you can be imprisoned in the worst abuse, or locked in the most sophisticated jail, and God can break through anything to speak to and comfort you.

It wasn't until my mid to late teens that I began to realize that my mother's struggle was primarily mental, because when her "angry phase" would pass, she was the most amazing, selfless, hard-working woman I knew, and I would often say that Mom was one of my best friends. Her weaknesses didn't turn me against her—Dad's emphasis on seeing the good in people combined with my own understanding of human worth drawn from the scriptures, taught me how to love someone in spite of their struggles. Sometimes I lost my temper in frustration, but I always tried to apologize and make reparation.

Deep inside, I felt there was something deeper behind Mom's emotional and mental "ups and downs," and taking the time to ponder and pray helped me to forgive her and move forward. The heart of the Gospel is *forgiveness*. God had forgiven me of *so many* faults, weaknesses, and mistakes—how could I turn and not follow His example? As the years have passed, I have used the experiences from *every* trial I have ever had to serve others with greater wisdom and insight.

However, as the years passed, Mom declined. The low points began falling deeper, and they became more frequent. It became more and more difficult to resist the anger and not fight back. Mom eventually left my Dad. At first, for over a month and a half, Dad pursued no legal action or involvement of attorneys. He just wanted peace. Friends warned that Mom was likely pursuing legal action herself, although she claimed she didn't want a divorce. It is a common tactic in divorce situations, and a few friends even sent recommendations for legal counsel, but Dad wouldn't budge. Finally, the day came when he was formally alerted that our friends were right. She had been pursuing legal action, and he was late in the game, but he didn't seem to mind. His trust was in the Lord. His voice was first for peace, and he felt confident the Lord would help.

Mom made all manner of false accusations and serious charges, even criminal, against Dad to ensure he would rarely, if ever, see his own kids again, but Dad wouldn't lose his confidence in the Lord. He knew the truth and he knew that God was in control.

The Lord knew the way through the wilderness. All we had to do was follow. We sang hymns and folk songs together each night, and we even prepared for and spoke at an expo during this time. We held family scripture study every day and even discovered game changing research on the Doctor Philastus Hurlbut story (later published in *Seer Stone v. Urim & Thummim*). We started to empathize with some of Joseph Smith's legal experiences in a new way.

We did what was necessary on the legal end, but miracles and 'coincidental' events occurred often. Two months later, instead of heading to trial, the matter was unexpectedly wrapped up, and Dad ended up with joint legal and physical custody—the three youngest children lived equally in both homes, but our two teenage brothers were given the choice to live where they wanted. Isaiah and Ephraim had already left Mom and moved back in with Dad after episodes of emotional and/or physical abuse, and they continued to choose Dad's home full time to the day he passed away.

Unfortunately, Mom's struggles involved serious delusional and sociopath-like behaviors. Even strange uncontrolled actions involving stolen items occurred. She began spreading false rumors and trying to do everything she could to stir people up against Dad and our family. Some friends felt she was intentionally lying, but from my experience and perspective, it seemed more of a delusion she genuinely believed.

But that didn't stop the false slander. She told stories about how her own children were angry and uneducated, that James Stoddard starved and physically abused his children, that she was never allowed to be a mother during their marriage, that Dad had visions of a "great earthquake" wiping out Salt Lake City following which he would become the next prophet, that Dad made Mom pray to him, and the stories just got more and more colorful. The narrative sounded like a Warren Jeffs conspiracy 2.0. She even made accusations against Leah's and my moral virtue and chastity. Oh, that hurt in ways I can never describe in words. She stalked Leah, some friends of ours, and myself on Facebook; and at one point, she even accused Isaiah of possibly molesting Eliza, leading to an investigation that found absolutely no support for any such claims. Isaiah was vindicated—but the experience was traumatic, especially when it came from his own mother.

Those who knew our family knew the truth, but what about all the strangers who didn't? I would get accusatory emails and messages. Once I got a letter from someone who claimed to 'love' us and then angrily ranted for 12 pages repeating all of Mom's lies. Did this person care to know the truth? No. I just had to ignore the aggressive attackers and move on.

At one point, I became so angry from taking it and taking it that I decided enough was enough. I wanted to fight back—to tell the truth! I was angry, and I didn't know what to do, so fortunately I got down on my knees and prayed, "*What should I do Lord?*" I thought, "*He is smart. He can think of a great strategy!*" Instead, the answer came calmly and gently: "*Build up the good. Lift, don't tear down.*"

I was a little dumbfounded, but I knew without a shadow of doubt He was right. They were the words Dad had taught us repeatedly growing up. "There are two kinds of people in this world," he would often say. "People who do good, and people who talk and gossip about people who do good. Always lift and build. Always." So I shut my mouth and went to work building 'good.' We started a pilot program for families called "Raising the Bar," we gave firesides on Church history and music principles, I wrote a standards curriculum, and we published our first book, *Seer Stone v. Urim & Thummim!*

Then one day, I hit another wall of frustration, and I wanted to privately confront Mom. So I wrote an email. I didn't pray through it this time though! Oh dear. I expressed my frustration and demanded the truth. I listed instance after instance where she had lied, and I could prove it. I was about to send this epistle when Dad walked by, and I made the wise 'mistake' of telling him what I was up to. He looked me steadily in the eye, and simply commented, "You sound angry."

"*Wow, brilliant insight, Dad!*" I thought. "*Yeah, surprised you figured that out. Yes, I am.*" Verbally, I just said, "Ummm, well . . ."

Dad looked at me calmly but searchingly. "Are you trying to get back at her, or are you trying to *help* her?"

"Dad!" I protested, "She doesn't want help. She doesn't care what I think, and she believes she is perfect. She sends 'nice' emails literally on the same days she is harassing and stabbing us behind our backs!"

"Maybe right now," he said gently. "But what about in the future? What about some time when something clicks, and she is desperate for a friend, for a chance to have a relationship with her kids or someone who can help her? Will she know you are there? She needs to know you will be there to help."

I gulped. I wanted to give some clever rebuttal, but I couldn't. I knew he was right, so I bit my lip, slowly turned around to my laptop and started hitting the backspace key.

A couple of days later, I sent a different email. Perfect? Probably not, but my best for a 25-year-old wading through parental betrayal and public slander. But Dad's guiding question never left me: "Are you trying to help her?"

My Mom pursued legal action against Dad pretty consistently over the years, but her attempts to pull the kids away from him were not successful. Through it all, I learned a very important lesson. There is suffering in the world, and sometimes people make poor choices that hurt innocent people—even children—but although God does not, and cannot, take away the trial, He *always* helps those who rely on him to get through it. Am I a better person today because of these experiences? Yes. Is my family better equipped to help others? Yes, in ways we had never dreamed! People began coming to us and sharing experiences and stories they had been reluctant to share with others, but now they felt that we could understand. We had empathy born of suffering. I began to see my life in an entirely different way. Jesus Christ is able to succor each of us, because he has experience, He knows exactly what we are feeling. Likewise, we gain *experience* so we can succor others, following in His steps.

"What About My Kids?": Hannah & Leah

What was the secret to not becoming bitter—to becoming *better* and remaining unbroken through trials? The Gospel of Jesus Christ taught by a faithful father.

Dad was hurt, but he wouldn't become bitter. Dad wanted to be angry, but he prayed, and God gave him love for Mom even when she kept firing back. Sometimes when Dad got snarky text messages, he just wouldn't respond. He patiently turned to the Lord, even as his heart was breaking, and asked, *What do you want me to do now?*

FORGIVENESS

Leah remembers: Dad had the most beautiful ability to forgive, more than anyone I have ever met. He forgave my mistakes, moved on, and didn't bring them up again. Dad *never* sat around and bashed on people who had injured him. He really didn't! I watched him respond with love. He followed the scripture, "Therefore if thine enemy hunger, feed him; if he thirst, give him drink." (Romans 12:20) Actually, *literally*; he offered her free goat milk and well water after she left, and gave her whatever food and kitchenware items she wanted from our house. Not out of bribery—that was never in his nature—only kindness. He'd receive so many spiteful messages and emails, but he'd always respond in a level-headed way, without any ulterior motive than calmly addressing the concerns. I have watched my Dad carefully and as objectively as possible throughout my entire life to see if he *really* believed and lived what he taught us. He did.

At one point, Dad was praying about his kids, worried about the trauma and hardships they were going through. This wasn't fair! "*What about my kids, Lord?*" He asked.

The simple, but life-changing, answer came: "James, what about <u>MY</u> kids?" Everyone around us: the struggling family in the ward, the homeless mother wandering the inner city, the underage pregnant teen scared in an abortion clinic, the high schooler sitting alone on the bus planning how to end his life, the returned missionary who lost his faith and was angrily turning in his resignation to the Church—these were all the Lord's kids, and He loved them just as much as Dad loved his little children. What about the Lord's kids? Would we turn outside our private grief and love God's children enough to rally our team again—laying down our grief to serve?

It wasn't an easy step to take, but as a family, we got on our knees and said, "yes." It was time to go back to work.

CHAPTER
Sixteen

"THE ANSWER IS ON YOUR DRESSER"
ISAIAH'S CONVERSION

*"If any man will do his will, he shall know of the doctrine,
whether it be of God, or whether I speak of myself."*

— John 7:17

*This chapter is written by Isaiah regarding his experience
gaining a testimony and witness for himself.*

W hen I was a kid I didn't care very much about the Gospel. It took a bit longer for me than for others to understand how important it really is. One of my favorite memories from when I was young was when my Dad would take the time to read with me from the scriptures or from an illustrated Church History series that we had. I thought the stories were interesting, and with Dad, it was never boring—but I didn't really understand *why* they were so important.

I was very young when our family got started with the projects that eventually became the Joseph Smith Foundation. When I got a bit older, I started helping with simple jobs. I was glad that I was able to help with something important, but it still felt like just another 'to do' on the list. In my mind, it was similar to weeding the yard—it was just another thing I had to do before I could do something more fun.

The Book of Mormon says that a gift given grudgingly is counted the same as if that person had retained the gift. (Moroni 7:8) At that time in my life, my support of Gospel projects and the vision of service that my Dad had started was definitely given grudgingly. I did it because it was the 'right' thing to do, and not because I wanted to follow the Savior. Dad always told us that it was very important for each of us to receive our own testimony of the Gospel and the Restoration. He would say that when the fight gets hard and the "sunshine patriots" have left, the only people who would remain would be those who were driven by their own personal testimonies from the inside. Heber C. Kimball once prophesied that:

> The time will come when no man nor woman will be able to endure on borrowed light. Each will have to be guided by the light within himself. If you do not have it, how can you stand? . . .
>
> You will be left to the light within yourselves. If you don't have it you will not stand; therefore seek for the testimony of Jesus and cleave to it, that when the trying time comes you may not stumble and fall.[1]

That "time" was soon coming for me and my siblings—but right then, it was easier to just procrastinate and have fun. That proved to be one of the biggest mistakes I have ever made.

If anyone had asked, I would have said that I did believe in the Restoration and the scriptures, but that answer was only based on tangible evidence. Being in a home where the Gospel was always discussed—and having attended events such as the Book of Mormon Evidence Conference—I had seen the facts supporting the Book of Mormon, the life of Christ, and the Restoration. I 'believed' in the Church, but I hadn't put in the work to have the spiritual witness.

---

1   Orson F. Whitney, *Life of Heber C. Kimball* (Salt Lake City: Kimball Family, 1888), 461.

Isaiah & Ephraim unloading a mower at our homestead

Learning to Work

When I was around ten, our family purchased a piece of rocky, sagebrush-covered property in Sanpete County, Utah. Our goal was to heal the land using natural methods that God organized. It was on this property that my Dad taught me one of the most important lessons that I have ever learned—how to work. We spent pretty much every weekend—and often multiple weekdays—working on that property. We built a fence, put in irrigation systems, planted thousands of plants, and built a shop. Being able to work alongside my Dad was one of the greatest blessings I have ever had. I learned so much, not only from the skills he taught us, but also from the way that I saw him approach and figure out problems—one day at a time. Some days the weather wasn't the best, or we were tired—but looking back I only regret not working harder, and I wouldn't exchange those experiences for anything. My Dad would tell us that when we looked back we wouldn't ever regret being *too good*, or not sinning enough, but instead, we would regret our shortcomings—and he was right.

Facing a Crossroad

When I was 15, my Mom decided to leave my Dad. My Mom had us load up in the car one day on the premise of going to the park. Instead, we were taken to live with my Mom away from my Dad and older siblings. At first, things were okay, but they began to rapidly deteriorate. The standards at the home we now lived in were much lower than those we had lived growing up. Pretty soon, I realized that my Mom could no longer be someone that I trusted or looked to as a source for truth. I realized that just like my Dad had said, the day had come when we could no longer rely on the testimony of others for our support. I realized that I was now the oldest sibling in that home, and not only was I responsible for myself, but also for my younger brothers and sisters. My siblings would be looking to me for an example, and I could no longer afford to be wrong. Each of us had come to a crossroad. We could either continue to live the more difficult and unpopular standards that we had grown up with, or we could take the path of least resistance and live for ourselves.

As time passed, things continued to get steadily worse. Every day, Mom's anger would intensify and be poured out all around the house. My Mom also began to suffer in other mental ways. We began to hear new 'stories' spreading around about how we had been abused by my Dad, and that my Dad had started a cult where he was essentially the new god. At first, my siblings and I did not know that these stories were being told about us—my Mom was careful that we were never present when these stories were told—otherwise we would have seen through them, but gradually we began to figure it out.

"The Answer is On the Dresser"

One day I came across a couple of messages from my Mom, and I was pretty stunned not only by the extent to which the stories were taken, but also by the straight-faced way in which these falsehoods were told. I started digging a bit deeper, and pretty quickly I realized that there were more imaginative stories around every corner. My first reaction was that it was sort of silly, and that nobody would really believe my Mom or the tales she was claiming had actually happened, but I began to see more and more people who actually believed her.

That night, I was pretty mad at my Mom. I could kind of understand someone who twists a story for their own purpose, but I wondered how someone could just generate a story out of thin air claiming that someone is guilty of some of the worst things a person can do. I had no idea where to begin or how to approach this.

As I said my prayers that night, I asked for help to understand what I was supposed to do and how I was supposed to confront these issues. Almost immediately, I felt one of the most powerful feelings that I have ever felt. It was almost like someone said, *"the answer is on the dresser."* I thought I was just imagining things so I just kept praying. A couple of seconds later, the same thing was repeated again—but it was a lot more powerful. *"The answer is on the dresser!"* This time I knew 100 percent that there was no way I could have possibly imagined that. I thought, *"Dresser? What's on the dresser?"* I tried to remember what was on the dresser, but I couldn't.

Over in the corner of the bedroom there was a wooden dresser that was about four feet tall. It had four drawers and was painted red, white, and blue. I started to stand up, and immediately I saw what was on top of the dresser: a book that I'm sure everyone reading this has seen before. It's a small, blue book with gold lettering on the front. There on my dresser was a copy of the Book of Mormon that had been given to me before I was baptized. I opened it up randomly, and the first verse that caught my eye was on the middle right side near the bottom. It was 3 Nephi 12:44, which reads:

But behold I say unto you, love your enemies, bless them that curse you, do good to them that hate you, and pray for them who despitefully use you and persecute you . . . (3 Nephi 12:44)

It was a little frightening, but as soon as I read those words, I knew what I needed to do. When I started my prayer, I had been very angry at my Mom—but now I felt sorry for her and wanted to think of ways to help her. I realized that I was no different than her. The anger that I had felt before beginning my prayer was the same exact feeling that had led my Mom to where she currently was.

I wrote the verse down on a little piece of paper and pinned it on the wall where I could see it from my bed. Ever since then, it has been my favorite chapter and verse in the scriptures. I can't say that I have always felt forgiving toward my Mom since that experience—but when I do get frustrated, I try to remember that night and bring back that spirit of forgiveness. I often think that choosing to forgive isn't just a battle—it's much harder than a battle.

The heart of the Gospel is forgiveness and charity.

Praying to Discover My Mission

That was the night I received my initial spiritual witness of the Book of Mormon and the Restoration. I realized for the first time that I needed to give up what I wanted to do, and instead do what God wanted me to do. In the *Lectures on Faith*, which the Prophet Joseph Smith is believed to have helped put together in Kirtland, it teaches that "a religion that does not require the sacrifice of all things, never has power sufficient to produce the faith necessary unto life and salvation." It continues by saying:

" It is in vain for persons to fancy to themselves that they are heirs with those, or can be heirs with them, who have offered their all in sacrifice, and by this means obtained faith in God and favor with him so as to obtain eternal life, unless they in like manner offer unto him the same sacrifice, and through that offering obtain the knowledge that they are accepted of him.[2]

I decided that it was time to stop acting like a conscript, and raise the banner of Jesus Christ for myself—not because someone said that I had to, or because I was tricked into it, but because I knew that it was the path that God wanted me to follow and that it would bring joy. In the Doctrine and Covenants, it says that we should "cheerfully do all things that lie in our power," with "great earnestness," even if it requires wasting and wearing out our lives, and then we may "stand still, with the utmost assurance, to see the salvation of God, and for his arm to be revealed." (Doctrine & Covenants 123:17) I was determined to follow through, no matter how hard it would get. I thought that if I sacrificed enough, then God might be able to use me to eventually help my Mom.

I quickly realized that God's way is very narrow, and that there is only one way to salvation. If there are 365 different directions I could potentially go in, only one is the right way. I knew that I wouldn't be able to serve two masters. I was either going to be all in, or all out. I decided to commit to giving it my best shot.

Latter-day prophets have taught us that every person has specific missions that they have previously agreed to perform in the premortal life. I decided to get down right then and pray to know what those missions were—and I received answers. Over the next few days, God opened my eyes a little bit, and I was able to understand some of them. They really were right in front of me the entire time, I just didn't see them until I asked. The reason I share this is to help others know that they can have

---

2 *Lectures on Faith*, Lecture 6.

the same experience. If you commit to sacrifice what you'd like to do for His will, then He will let you know what He wants accomplished. It will probably surprise you just how many things there are to do.

‿⁀

The Lord will reveal your mission if you ask.

‿⁀

Returning Home

I wish I could say that things got better after this—but instead they took a deep plunge for the worse. My Mom's mental struggles and anger towards my Dad continued to increase, and anyone who mentioned anything positive about my Dad got picked on. Exactly two months after my Mom left, I left her house and returned to live with my Dad. It was hard to leave my siblings on their own, but the environment was not healthy and I knew it was the right thing to do.

One of the lessons I learned from this is that testimonies come from doing hard things. The Savior was perfect, but He had the hardest life. What does that tell us if we expect to follow Him? Moroni says that we receive no witness until after the *trial* of our faith. (Ether 12:6) I had to live the principle of sacrifice of my own accord before I was able to get a testimony of it, and that testimony isn't static—it continues to either grow or shrink all the time depending on how well I live the commandments. I don't think that I would have been able to do it if my Dad hadn't taught me the lessons of work, discipline, and obedience as we worked on our property in Sanpete County.

Hard things also teach us how reliant we are on God. Sometimes it might seem like we are doing fine on our own and that we don't need Him, but King Benjamin teaches us in the Book of Mormon that we rely on God to support us every moment of the day, and that even if we were to serve him with all our souls, we would still be unprofitable servants. (Mosiah

2:21) How many times do we thank God for allowing us to breathe? It's only when we are not able to breathe anymore that we can fully realize how we took that blessing for granted all along. In the same way, I didn't realize how blessed I was to have a Dad who taught us the Gospel, and whom we could look to for an example—until I didn't have that anymore.

A testimony and sure witness comes from taking the harder road and sacrificing.

God's Plan Cannot Be Frustrated

Another lesson I learned is that God's plans cannot be frustrated. Whenever someone tries to get in the way or make trouble, God uses that to our advantage. In 1838, Joseph Smith and five other church leaders spent the winter locked up on false charges in a dark, cold jail with barely enough 'food' to keep them alive. But while in the middle of it, God told Joseph Smith that "all these things shall give thee experience, and shall be for thy good." (Doctrine & Covenants 122:7) There are things that we can learn through hard times that we cannot learn any other way. This is one of the reasons why we are commanded to "Rejoice evermore" and "in every thing give thanks." (1 Thessalonians 5:16, 18) Like Joseph in Egypt, God will use everything that happens for His purposes, and to build up His kingdom. Because of these trials, I feel like I can use my experiences to help others. This is the important lesson that I began to learn while separated from my Dad.

It doesn't stop there though. It takes a constant renewal to keep going and stay on the path. We need to expect things to get harder—because they *will*. Satan is constantly analyzing us for our vulnerabilities. It's not enough to have a testimony of the Gospel in just one area. Our testimony is like a chain that is only as strong as its weakest link. Our defense system against the attacks of Satan is only as strong as its weakest point, and he always goes for that one spot. Pretty quickly, we will all realize that we can't make it on our own. It's only when we put our trust in the Master that we can gain true success.

We need to use every free moment as preparation for the trials that are coming. The prophet Alma asks: "If ye have experienced a change of heart, and if ye have felt to sing the song of redeeming love, I would ask, can ye feel so now?" Our testimony will never be static, and we are always moving either forward or backwards. The promise is there: "if any man will do his will, he shall know of the doctrine, whether it be of God, or whether I speak of myself." (John 7:17) I can testify that this is true.

Another lesson that my Dad would often remind us of is that we have already committed to follow Christ. If you have been

From left to right: Hannah, Leah, cousin Mary, Ephraim, and Isaiah

baptized, it's not a matter of *when* you will decide to follow Christ—the fact is that we already have, and we renew that covenant every week as we partake of the sacrament. If we pay close attention to the prayers offered over the sacrament, it's quite clear what we are committing to do. Every time we partake of the sacrament we commit to:

- *Take upon us the name of Christ.* We are committing to do exactly what He would do if He were here.

- *Always remember Him.* Christ must be always in our minds. We need to build our life around the Gospel instead of just fitting it in wherever we can.

- *Keep His commandments.* We are committing to keep every commandment that we have been given so that we can keep the Spirit of Christ with us.

I think that we often forget what a serious ordinance the sacrament is. Every time we partake, we are committing to deny

Isaiah & siblings with Rod Meldrum during joint speaking event

ourselves and "take up his cross."[3] It's not something to be taken lightly.

However, if we continue in righteousness, and endure to the end, we will be rewarded. King Benjamin reminds us that we should consider "the blessed and happy state of those that keep the commandments of God." He promises that we will be "blessed in all things, both temporal and spiritual." (Mosiah 2:41) The Savior taught that "whosoever will save his life shall lose it: and whosoever will lose his life for my sake shall find it." (Matthew 16:25)

This is what our Dad wanted us to always remember. Like Abraham, we can also come to understand for ourselves that there is greater happiness, peace, and rest in following Christ. Knowing this, we should not be discouraged—but instead, we should rejoice and proclaim with Joseph Smith:

 Brethren, shall we not go on in so great a cause? Go forward and not backward. Courage, brethren; and on, on to the victory! (Doctrine & Covenants 128:22)

---

3 JST, Matthew 16:25-26; Doctrine & Covenants 56:2; Mark 8:34; Luke 9:23.

CHAPTER
Seventeen

FINDING CONFIDENCE AGAIN

*"Let thy bowels also be full of charity towards all men,
and to the household of faith, and let virtue garnish thy
thoughts unceasingly; then shall thy confidence wax
strong in the presence of God . . ."*

— *Doctrine & Covenants 121:45*

S eer Stone v. Urim & Thummim was a *complete* miracle.
While the research was conducted over a few years, the
entire book was written and prepared for publication in
about two months—all while homeschooling and reorganizing
our finances. Dad was still working full time as a software
engineer and our family was still reeling after the traumatic year
before. To this day, we still aren't sure how it happened. We
weren't even planning on it in January. We were on the phone
with a good friend who suddenly said, "Would you guys please
write a book on the translation? We really need your research
documented, and we can't wait forever. And can you have it
ready for the Book of Mormon Evidence Expo in April?" Dad
looked at us, we looked at Dad, and at the same moment, we all
knew in our heart what we were supposed to do. Were we crazy?
That wasn't even a question.

Dad was heartbroken and traumatized by the divorce. After
those experiences, his health problems worsened, and he

Leah working on footnotes & research

never regained his strength. He loved our Mom until the day he died, and the emotional and physical toll was too much. While writing *Seer Stone v. Urim & Thummim*, his health continued to go downhill as he continued to care for the little kids, guiding his teen boys full time, and keeping up with his software job. He never saw the manuscript until after it was delivered to the printer, because he was too sick to continue using the computer after his career work was finished. All of his writing and subsequent edits to the manuscript were done *orally*. Dad would dictate while resting on the couch or in a chair, and Hannah would read and reread the chapters aloud. At night, we would gather the family and listen to each chapter, offering suggestions. Leah designed the cover and helped Isaiah (15 years old), Ephraim (13 years old), Mary (10 years old), and Ezra (7 years old) lay out the interior.

Dad's weakness turned out to be a blessing in disguise. As our family set out to write the book, friends rallied to help us accomplish the impossible. Grandma Stoddard was a continual source of strength, encouragement, wisdom, and temporal support. Friends volunteered countless hours in the wee hours of the morning, and long after everyone else had gone to bed, to

Eliza helping ship Seer Stone v. Urim & Thummim orders

help edit, research, review, and give other contributions. When the book was finally finished, everyone on the team walked away with stronger testimonies and spiritual experiences born of sacrifice. It was a milestone for our family—and a testimony that even in the midst of adversity, the Lord does prevail!

Faith Crisis, Volume 1: We Were NOT Betrayed! was another adventure. Dad was feeling better this time, but the kids had a bad case of flu during the writing period. Passing by one of the bedrooms, one would have seen Hannah typing away with her hair up in a ponytail, and kids lying on her lap hugging a pan. We'd get someone a drink of water, type a few lines, go clean up an accident on the carpet, type a few more paragraphs, and the cycle would continue. Life carried on and we worked around it! Hannah was weaker during this time and wanted to give up on multiple occasions, but Dad kept us all motivated and going! We learned to prioritize family prayer, lots of walks outside, and trips to the park to play wiffle ball, tag, and soccer to stay sane and maintain balance.

Sera, 22-year-old friend, remembers: I was blessed to spend some time in James Stoddard's home—working on a website and other projects—wherein there would be plenty of laughter and jokes as we pegged away. During this time of darkness for the family after a bitter divorce, I felt the most amazing spirit still and the consecration of time and talents continued to fill their home.

There was a good amount of work that needed to be finished, such as chores and animals to take care of, but there were also times for play that he insisted on doing as a family. There would be times we were at the park and James would join in on the fierce game of basketball or kickball, and then there were other times when Ezra would start wrestling him and he would finish the match by quickly pinning him.

I wholeheartedly enjoyed these visits and watching how the family interacted with one another—all the jokes and sarcasm throughout all the ups and downs of the work that was being done never ceased. My favorite memory was when he would grab young Eliza and participate in Old English dancing as her partner. The connection between fatherhood and friendship was taught and displayed many times on my visits. I learned that when good men take up the mantle of fatherhood, they enter into a calling that has a transformative impact well beyond their own joy and happiness. I know because it transformed, for good, my life and view of a father forever.

During this time, a touching moment occurred with our sister Mary (nearly 11 years old at the time). Mary followed Ephraim's example and became absolutely obsessed with chickens—especially fluffy silkies or Chinese silk chickens. She begged and pleaded for us to purchase a flock of hens, some chicks, and build her a coop. She and Ephraim talked about their new enterprise constantly, reading books and participating in online forums. Mary wanted to start in late winter—early spring of 2020, but we were in the middle of finishing *Faith Crisis, Volume 1*. Ephraim and Mary couldn't bear to wait and were secretly concocting a plan to wake up early one morning, bike two miles to the nearest Tractor Supply store, purchase a set of chicks and then 'surprise' us all when they magically appeared near our goat pen. When the bikes mysteriously broke, they decided to walk. If you know one thing about Stoddards, they are determined and they don't take 'no' for an answer.

However, one afternoon, Hannah, Leah and Mary sat down and had a heart-to-heart conversation about timing and the fact that if they tried to start the chicken business now, we wouldn't be able to finish the book because of time constraints. Could Mary please wait until mid to end of April? In Mary's own words, "It was a *dreadful* conversation." It was hard for her young 11-year-old heart to delay her dream, even for a few months, and she was seeing listing after listing on KSL of great deals to get hens. Mary agreed, however, that if we all put the Lord first and did His project, the Lord would open opportunities for us to get all the hens we needed when the time was right. So, we put the chicken project on the shelf. A few months later, when the book was finished, everything miraculously fell into place to get the chickens we needed. Someone near Salt Lake decided to sell two of their golden silkies for a cheap price, and even offered to bring them half-way. Then, an unexpected disaster-turned-miracle prompted us to move our livestock to a new piece of property that was a hundred times better than the old location! It was an important lesson for the kids in priorities, timing, and patience.

Bonding As Siblings

Through each success or failure that came our way, our bond as siblings seemed to grow stronger, creating a productive 'team.' As siblings, we have always loved each other and have seen ourselves as a united band—sometimes for good, often for mischief. Sometimes, we took life a little *too* seriously as we banded together to dispel any real or imagined threat that came our way. To illustrate this point, we have to go back in time for a moment. Hannah, James, and Leah were often the chief sibling ringleaders, dubbing themselves "The Three Musketeers." For example, one evening Dad went grocery shopping after he

Finally! The day to buy the chickens arrived!

got home from work. Mom was sick in her room and in the darkness, our united imaginations—dangerous enough on their own but when joined together they could invent even more serious drama—began suspecting our home could be robbed at any time. Threats were no joke and we *would* defend the home front, come what may. James (around 7-years-old) led the way as we gathered Dad's big metal baseball bats from the garage, rope, and other household objects. Urgently, we began planning a set of booby traps and decoys for the criminals we were sure would be appearing at any moment. When we heard the sound of the garage door opening, a scream of "Dad's home!! Clean everything up FAST!" echoed through the house. Everything was replaced when he came in . . . except for the baseball bats.

Dad was really confused: "What on earth are those doing by the door?" Shrugging our shoulders, we quietly grabbed them and scampered off to the garage.

Another time, we were wrestling and having a pillow fight in our family room while Dad and Mom were on an afternoon walk. Now, we weren't *supposed* to be rambunctious in that room—hence why Dad literally installed a mini gym in our basement with padded floors, walls, a basketball hoop, etc. But . . . we weren't always the most obedient. As we screamed and tussled with each other in delight, someone hit a Christmas snow globe sitting on a side table, and we watched in horror as it crashed to the ground and shattered—glitter, glass, and liquid spreading across the carpet. What were we going to do?! We huddled together in an emergency brainstorming session, and finally concluded we had committed a serious 'sin.' Dad and Mom were about to discover our crimes, and since we had been taught that serious transgressions should be confessed to the bishop, we immediately began searching for the ward directory. Fortunately, just as we were dialing his number—our fingers hovering over the buttons—we were interrupted by Dad and Mom walking in the door. Oh how they laughed! We just looked at each other confused.

Of course, we as siblings struggled with the common challenges of sibling rivalry and conflicting personalities. We went through rough places in our friendships. Some siblings seemed to get along naturally; others struggled. Because we were united as a family to accomplish a mission, because the Gospel was the center, and because we were taught to be loyal and true— regardless of age or personality differences—we were eventually able to work through all of these challenges.

As time passed, the toddlers Hannah and Leah had chased around in diapers became young men and women who were essential and integral parts of our team. Isaiah and Ephraim became brothers we looked up to, both in height and character, with respect and appreciation. While they both had some serious rascal phases in their youth, their creativity and love for adventure began to be used for good as they gained their own

Ephraim working with our citation team on a book project

personal conversion to the Gospel of Jesus Christ. Instead of creating science experiments, they channeled that energy into the Lord's cause.

Ephraim was the cheerful, sympathetic, loving friend you couldn't help but feel uplifted just to be around. He would always stick up for the underdog, and was willing to make any sacrifice to help a younger sibling. His smile would brighten anyone's dark day! He started his own chicken business, Peeps & Eeps, and would never hesitate to hop on social media and engage in debates: battling for Joseph Smith or the Restoration.

As our Joseph Smith Foundation team began working on piloting our new Raising the Bar program, Ephraim discovered his love for writing and often contributed his own insights as seen by the following post he wrote entirely by himself:

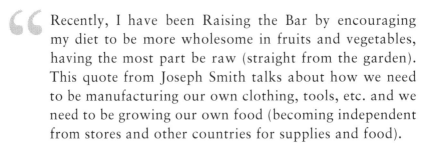

Recently, I have been Raising the Bar by encouraging my diet to be more wholesome in fruits and vegetables, having the most part be raw (straight from the garden). This quote from Joseph Smith talks about how we need to be manufacturing our own clothing, tools, etc. and we need to be growing our own food (becoming independent from stores and other countries for supplies and food).

... let all those who appreciate the blessings of the Gospel, and realize the importance of obeying the commandments of heaven ... first prepare for the general gathering; let them dispose of their effects as fast as circumstances will possibly admit, without making too great sacrifices, and remove to our city and county; establish and build up manufactures in the city, purchase and cultivate farms in the county.... (Joseph Smith, Proclamation to the Saints Scattered Abroad (1841) Presidents Joseph & Hyrum Smith, and Sidney Rigdon)

After reading this quote from Joseph Smith, I asked myself, how can I be more sustaining to myself and family as Joseph Smith wants/asks us to do? After thinking about it for some time I decided to have my diet become more wholesome with fruits, vegetables, herbs, and grains that come from our own garden. D&C Section 89, gives us a "word of wisdom" for the food we should be eating. Verse 10 tells us that "all wholesome herbs God hath ordained for the constitution, nature, and use of man." Also in verse 11, it tells us that we should be using "every" herb, fruit, vegetable, and grain "in the season thereof." This clearly explains to us that we need to use all the produce when it organically ripens so that the produce may be used with prudence and thanksgiving. God specially designated and designed these plants for us to "receive health in their navel and marrow to their bones; And shall find wisdom and great treasures of knowledge, even hidden treasures; And shall run and not be weary, and shall walk and not faint. And I, the Lord, give unto them a promise, that the destroying angel shall pass by them, as the children of Israel, and not slay them. Amen."

Here is a recipe for some of my salad ideas:

Greens enough for a main dish or side dish, perhaps a handful. Olive oil, Coconut oil (I have heard it can work but never tried coconut oil.)

Ezra is ready to work on book editing with his blue light glasses

Aged balsamic vinegar

Vegetables of choice: Carrots, cabbage, raw onions, turmeric, garlic, onion greens, lettuce, peppers, lovage, lemon sorrel, sprouts, seeds (hemp, sunflower, pumpkin, sesame), tomatoes, chives, fennel, horseradish, beet greens, radish, avocado, mushrooms, cilantro, parsley, salad Burnett, cucumbers, oregano, celery, broccoli, etc. Apples, Raisins, Nuts, Other things can be added of your own preference.

Meanwhile, Ezra (8-10 years old) became Dad's right hand man on projects, offering his critiques in a very authoritative tone on missing punctuation and "this part just doesn't make any sense." Once he was commenting in one of our Google Docs on a chapter for the Helen Mar Kimball biography and one of the editors messaged Hannah wondering who the new editor was. He sounded so assertive and sure of himself, they thought it must have been an adult—not little Ezra. We all got a good laugh that day!

In addition to becoming an expert at raising chickens and goats—and dazzling us with her incredible cooking skills—Mary (around 10-13 during this time) began studying out each standard and battleline for herself. She needed her own witness. Although she struggled naturally with writing and speaking, she pushed through and began sharing her own posts on social media and elsewhere:

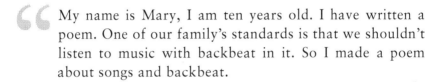 My name is Mary, I am ten years old. I have written a poem. One of our family's standards is that we shouldn't listen to music with backbeat in it. So I made a poem about songs and backbeat.

> *Oh, the melody is so sweet*
>
> *when it doesn't have that backbeat*
>
> *All the instruments playing,*
>
> *brings a peaceful feeling.*
>
> *My heart is always truly sad*
>
> *when songs turn that bad.*
>
> *But I am always greeting*
>
> *a song to praise our Lord and King.*

Family Loyalty

One of the adversary's greatest desires is to destroy the family and break the harmony that can ideally exist. If he breaks a family, he crushes a powerful force for good. Dad taught us the following principles in working together:

1. Your family should become your best friends. God put your family together for a reason. Stick together!

2. Be loyal to your team. They should never doubt that you have their back. Make sure they can count on you.

Mary's Poem

Oh, the melody is so sweet,
when it doesn't have that backbeat.
All the instruments playing,
brings a peaceful feeling.

My heart is always truly sad,
when songs turn that bad.
But I am always greeting
a song to praise our Lord and King.

3. Learn to forgive and love, even in the hardest situations. It is too easy to be nice to your friends and a jerk to those you live with. Family brings out your real character and level of charity. Use this measuring stick to improve!

4. Do not be ashamed to love, associate with, and enjoy your family.

All of us struggled at one point or another with periodic sibling rivalries or getting along with a conflicting personality, but each project brought our family closer. God is the only one who knows how to build a family, and His principles *work*. He has laws irrevocably decreed upon which all blessings are predicated, and His promises are <u>sure</u>. These principles had brought us success in the past—but they were about to be tested once again as we were unexpectedly hit with a tragedy for which we were entirely unprepared.

CHAPTER
Eighteen

A GOD OF MIRACLES

*". . . behold, I will show unto you a God of
miracles, even the God of Abraham, and the God
of Isaac, and the God of Jacob . . . God has not
ceased to be a God of miracles."*

— *Mormon 9:11, 15*

The day Dad collapsed was sudden and unexpected—
January 6, 2021. He had spent the day before with visitors
and that morning attended a neighborhood development
meeting. That afternoon, he couldn't get out of bed from what
we *thought* was an ulcer attack.

Dad had experienced many ulcer episodes—the unfortunate
aftermath from medications taken over 20 years before. Looking
back in retrospect, signs of deeper issues had been stealthily
creeping up on us for a few years, but Dad wasn't one to draw
attention to himself, and he was one of the toughest men we knew.
In other words, he wasn't honest about his discomfort, and he
had a high pain tolerance. Over the next month and a half, Dad
had increasing moments of intensifying pain and then days where
he seemed to improve. We weren't sure what the issue was—and
the fact that we had very limited insurance due to Dad losing his
software job in 2019, COVID-19 restrictions that would limit his
ability to see his kids or perhaps deny all visitors, past doctors who

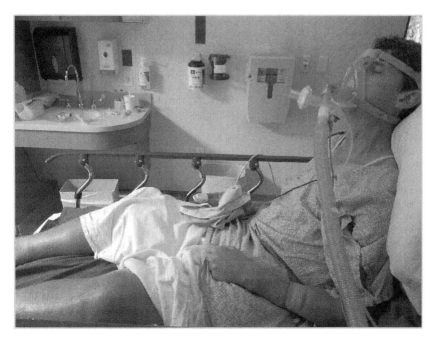

had struggled in vain to diagnose him and given up, and the fact that his system had experienced negative reactions to medications in the past—all led us to delay rushing to the hospital. Dad's bouts of illness and recurring pain were somewhat . . . normal in our home and none of us expected the explosive news we were about to receive.

Emergency Trip to the Hospital

Toward the end of February, Dad rapidly declined over a few days until he was having serious trouble breathing, swelling throughout his body, and an intense feeling of suffocation. However, he thought the pain was still ulcers and the side effects of being cooped up in bed without exercise. We tried some conventional solutions, but when he took a sharp turn for the worse—and a terrifying three days ensued—we called an ambulance and rushed him to the hospital. He was still mentally alert, but when he arrived, the hospital staff were *shocked*. His entire right lung had completely collapsed and his sodium level was 109 (what some consider incompatible with life). Dad! He

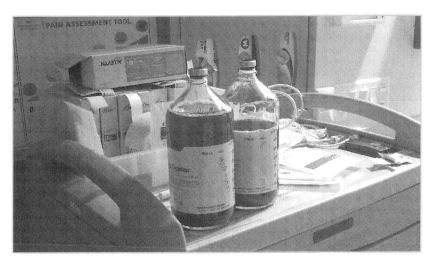

One sample of the effusion pulled the first day.

had not been upfront about how much pain he was really in and selflessly did not pay proper attention to very disturbing symptoms. Pericardial and pleural effusion, fluid around his heart and lungs, was present in large amounts—the worst some of them had ever seen. He was rushed to the ICU to begin having the fluid drained, and some of the doctors said they had never seen someone alive with such a low sodium level or that amount of fluid. He was in full cardiac tamponade. He should have been dead, but mysteriously . . . his heart was still beating, and he had not lost his mental clarity or cognizance.

They pulled 1.5 liters from his lung, 1.1 liters around his heart and over a liter from his bladder. Each liter weighed around 2.2 pounds. That first day, about 13 liters were pulled in approximately 12 hours. As the swelling came down, we were *shocked* to see how thin he was—he looked like he had walked out of a concentration camp. Beginning the process of balancing his electrolytes, pulling the fluid, trying to lower the swelling throughout the rest of his body and then determining the root cause was an extremely delicate balance.

At this point, Hannah hadn't slept for 72 hours. When the ambulance took Dad to the hospital, a close friend (a former ICU nurse) took her to the Provo hospital—giving her 20 minutes to release the emotions pent up over the last little while—and gear up for what was coming. When they arrived, she said goodbye and prepared to enter alone, only to discover another *huge* miracle! That very day the hospital had literally *just* changed their policy to allow two visitors. Words cannot express the relief this gave us as this nurse was able to go in the hospital with Hannah to give emotional support and assist as a patient advocate for Dad. God was literally in every detail, and when Dad finally fell asleep that night, we all cried with joy.

True to Dad's character, as soon as he was able to breathe again and in between sleeping in the night, his cheerful attitude brightened the hospital room. Before he could even talk, he would shakily write out messages to family on a piece of paper and his first comment was: "CRAZY!!!" (referring to this hospital adventure). The next comments? "How are you guys feeling?" "Tell [our friend] thank you." "Make sure you get yourself some treats." "Stop worrying about me." As soon as the BIPAP breathing aid came off, he was making light-hearted jokes with the nurses and doctors, starting Gospel conversations with those who were Latter-day Saints, and even talked for a little while with someone who was struggling with their hope and testimony. He was on the brink of death but his passion could not be dampened. Soon, he was cranking his head backwards to watch the vital signs monitor, wanting to understand everything that was going on and how it all worked. That was Dad! Never a dull moment and never content to sit back in ignorance—he always wanted to understand the how and why for everything around him.

The Cancer Diagnosis

Dad was already a walking and talking miracle and that first day, our friend noticed doctors from other floors in the hospital dropping by his room to observe. The next morning, however, and after an additional series of tests, it was discovered that Dad had stage 4 lung cancer, with tumors in his right lung and other concerning masses spread elsewhere. The tumors were advanced and malignant and had been growing for quite some time. As various doctors and specialists consulted, it was clear there was no medical solution. He should have already been dead, and the professionals were clear that he could be dead at any time—at the most he had a few months. They sent the hospital chaplain in to come and commiserate with Dad. You can guess how that conversation went . . . it may or may not have involved Joseph Smith's character, a review of the seer stone hypothesis, and traditionalist versus progressive history. Dad never wasted time.

We didn't have many conventional options so we started to see what could be done to get Dad as stable as possible to come home. The doctors put in a PleurX drainage catheter so we could drain his lung's pleural effusion ourselves. They wondered if it would be necessary to install a drain around the heart as well. Anything dealing with the heart is extremely dangerous, and this procedure would require staying longer in the hospital and limiting his activity at home. Miraculously, the fluid around the heart dropped off and on February 25, a sibling birthday, we all received the joyous news that Dad would be discharged the next day. Dad was in a lot of pain, but we just had to have faith and move forward a step at a time. We didn't really have conventional options for treating Dad's cancer, so we were left with whatever creative natural innovations we could discover. What did the Lord plan for the future? Who knew!

Our Thanksgiving Fast & Feast

When Dad got home, Isaiah and Ephraim helped carry him inside. Dad went straight for the sunroom built on the back of our house, basking in the fresh air and natural sunlight. We decided we would hold a fast and then a feast of thanksgiving with family and friends the next Sunday—one week away—to express our gratitude to God for his tender mercies and support. We even decided to do a musical sing-a-long over zoom! Hannah messaged our group of friends in the 'cancer update' thread:

 We were thinking this morning of Paul and Silas when they were flogged, beaten and imprisoned in Acts 16 and they spent the night chained in their cell SINGING praises to God. That was when the prison walls came down. No matter the current struggle, we have seen God fulfill His promises to deliver in the past and we have faith that this current obstacle (and more coming we do not know) will all be overcome and we feel like our family is going to set aside a day of thanksgiving and prayer praising God for all the mercy He has shown. We need to show God that we do acknowledge His plan, we do thank Him for ALL he has decreed in our life (the good and the bad) and we recognize that nothing can separate us from the love of Christ. We've united our faith together in pleading for help, now let's unite our faith in praising our God.

Over that week, Dad's energy, appetite, and strength began to improve, but we were worried about significant swelling that remained on his legs. A few days after coming home, we had a solemn family prayer, pleading with the Lord to intervene. The next day and the day after, the swelling began to go down. For our family, all of these events were a mammoth experience of faith based on obedience, prayer, and divine miracles.

Also, there was a prostate issue, likely an infection from a catheter in the hospital. During the night, the pain was severe enough that he couldn't sleep. When Saturday night came—the day before our 'Thanksgiving fast'—none of us felt like singing or being very grateful. Dad's prostate issues were still extremely painful, and he had been going without sleep for the most part. When Sunday morning came, we felt a heavy weight throughout our home. We had a choice to make: cry and complain to God, or put a smile on our faces and express gratitude for all the blessings we *had* received! We chose the latter option out of sheer grit. We *were* going to have our day of Thanksgiving.

That night, an incredible miracle took place when Dad was inspired with an idea that immediately began alleviating his prostate issue, and he was able to begin sleeping! We couldn't believe it! It was a humbling reminder to us to trust in the Lord's timing, avoid giving in to self-pity, and pressing forward with faith and gratitude.

⁓

"Pray without ceasing. In every thing give thanks . . ."

— *1 Thessalonians 5:7-8*

⁓

Going Back to Work

Nothing, not even stage 4 lung cancer, could keep Dad cooped up in the house. The next day, Dad walked one-third of a mile, and the day after that, he asked for his tablet and began checking up on where we were with the Joseph Smith Foundation and the battle for the Restoration online. Hannah messaged our friends' support thread:

> Things are looking up guys. My Dad is here catching up on/listening to [faith crisis podcasts] and planning out the Latter-day Answers vidcast. I told him this was off limits but . . . what could I do?? We watched *Facing the Giants* last night as well.

Life was a rollercoaster. We kept Dad's PleurX catheter drain free from infection and worked through random issues with kidney pain, anxiety, detox overload, and issues with fluid buildup. Step by step, we were inspired to find innovative and creative ways to help Dad sleep better. Sometimes, nothing we tried would work—but then we would pray, *again*, and a miracle would occur. One night, Dad was having trouble sleeping as usual, and past remedies failed over and over. He was praying when an idea came to mind. He tried it and . . . it worked! We soon realized this experience was not just about our faith, but also learning important lessons in health, nutrition, and healing that may be of benefit to others one day.

In the meantime, Dad used any free moments he had with the kids—working on projects with them. He helped Isaiah set up a new filming studio, and in May, filmed and edited a vidcast "Debunking *Rough Stone Rolling's* Treasure Digging Sources

At the hospital for an appointment

with REAL Data." He planned the outline for a few books, and supported Hannah in two podcast interviews. He also held regular scripture study with his kids—and one day in particular (March 21), challenged all of us to put God first in our life and focus all of our energy on serving others. Every afternoon he went walking, and neighbors occasionally came out to say, "What on earth are you doing, Brother Stoddard?? You are supposed to be in bed!"

Dad felt no assurance he would be healed, but he decided to make the most of the time he had and with faith and effort, live as long as it was God's will for his kids. It was painful—and he could have chosen at any time to go on strong painkillers and bring the suffering to a speedy end—but he deliberately chose to carefully avoid medications he knew would speed up the deterioration of his body. He told the Lord he was willing to go through any suffering required of him for the sake of his kids, and the Lord took him at his word. The suffering was intense, but the conversion experiences and the miracles we children witnessed during that time were profound.

The Miraculous May Fast

In May, Dad began a *fast* decline—and we weren't sure why—other than an effect of his overall cancer. He finally became so ill that we decided to go back to the emergency room. It was simply too dangerous to stay home. Hannah had been flat on her back with a severe migraine for two days, and so Dad said he would try to make it through the night. We would go to the hospital in the morning so she could rest. However, even more severe symptoms came, and at 9 p.m. we knew we needed to get to the hospital as soon as possible. In a providential answer to prayer, Hannah's pain became endurable just before we needed to go!

Unfortunately, after waiting hours and hours at the hospital to get some assistance, and after a series of tests, the doctor on staff essentially came in to inform us that Dad was dying and there was not much, if anything, they could do. They found what appeared to be a blood clot in his liver; they felt the cancer was spreading; his sodium level was only 113; there were signs of kidney failure, and a host of other issues. He could die that very night, they said, and he should be admitted into the hospital immediately to make him as comfortable as possible for the end. Dad had a decision to make. Due to COVID-19 policies, only two listed visitors were allowed, and this meant his kids could not come to say goodbye. If Dad wanted to see them again, he had to go home, but the doctors were adamantly against the idea. What should we do?

Dad thought for a moment and then faced the doctor with determination. "I'm not . . . staying here. If I only have . . . a few hours, . . . I'm going home . . . have to see my kids. . . . I'll come back . . . but I *have* to see them again."

Hannah drove Dad home. She had felt a confirmation that Dad was right—he needed to come home—but we didn't know what to expect. Nothing had been done at the hospital to relieve the pain of his symptoms so he was still in a lot of pain and could barely breathe. Once home, he rested for a little bit, but physically he could feel his system was shutting down—he was dying quickly. Tenderly, he called all of his kids who were home, along with his mother who was visiting, to give them a father's last counsel. We were all crying, trying to reconcile our wills to whatever God wanted. We filmed our Dad's message and then helped him rest in order to regain a little strength. It wasn't long before he got up and said, "We've got to get back to the hospital. I feel we just have to get back as soon as possible." He didn't have to ask Hannah twice—she readily agreed.

The return drive to Provo was difficult—every breath was a challenge. Hannah told us later that her vision really struggled from the migraine and tears that couldn't be held back. Thankfully, they didn't get in a car wreck. Before leaving, a friend messaged her, "You are at the same spot Joseph Smith was with his dad, or Brother Yun with his father.[1] This is when you must, as a family, offer your Dad to the Lord and trust Him like you never have before. This is your Abraham moment, your moment walking as God the Father did when He gave his own son: Complete submission having an assurance."

Once we arrived at the hospital, we realized the Lord had orchestrated everything with perfection. The staff this second time around was far better. They were helpful, creative, and ready to do whatever they could. A series of tests revealed large amounts of fluid around his heart and lungs again, and they went to work helping alleviate the symptoms. They drained 1700 ml from around his heart and another 1550 ml from around his right lung. We also providentially connected with an incredible cardiologist who would be a primary instrument in preserving Dad's life for the next three months. If it had not been for this second visit—separated by only a few hours from the first—Dad would have died months earlier and a significant amount of work and preparation would have been left undone. Dad walked out of the hospital on his own that afternoon, and for the first time in a long while, had the appetite for a good meal.

---

1   "Brother Yun" born 1958, is a Chinese Christian who served as an influential leader in the underground house church movement. When he was young, his father was deathly ill and almost died, but he was miraculously healed. This trial led their family to believe in Jesus Christ. See *The Heavenly Man: The Remarkable True Story of Chinese Christian Brother Yun*.

Meanwhile, a large fast had been organized and word began to spread. Friends and even supporters who had never met our family began fasting. As the fast began, we could literally feel the power and faith in our home. It was almost tangible—it is as vivid in our memory as if it happened yesterday. After a priesthood blessing from his brothers, Dad retired to rest—and then the biggest miracle of all took place. He slept . . . and slept . . . and slept. He slept for six hours without waking up! When he did wake up, he shortly after went back to sleep for another four hours! That was unheard of for him as far back as we could remember. Dad woke up without swelling, without numbness, and feeling like a new person. What did Dad do with his energy the next day? He was browsing online stores looking for film equipment we were missing in our studio. Dad just wouldn't give up!

*Never underestimate the power of
righteous prayer and fasting.*

We cried tears and tears of joy. Others fasted that Sunday, and once again, the power of faith could be felt in our home. We knew that no matter what the Lord had in store, He had never abandoned us. Dad's cancer was so advanced and so dangerous that most of the doctors consistently expressed the attitude, "Why would we do anything? You are just going to die within hours or days anyway," but the Lord was intervening to give Dad the time he needed to do whatever needed to be done.

Daily Challenges

There were good days, and there were bad days. This year was also the driest for Sanpete County since 1895 and water was scarce. In the midst of this drought, and with Dad out of commission, Isaiah and Ephraim took over our farm in Spring City on their own, working long hours in the heat to keep everything alive. Meanwhile, Hannah, Leah, Mary, and Ezra

The moment after Dad's heart rate finally came down and he found his Joseph Smith teachings book.

held down the homefront. In the midst of unexpected turns for the worse, we would send messages to friends for prayer and almost immediately, something or someone would appear for our good. At one point, everyone in the home got a very bad flu that included congestion, fever, body aches, and lung issues. We knew if Dad caught the bug, he would die. We prayed for him to be spared, and when he did come down with the illness, he curiously had every negative symptom *except* congestion or anything that would impact his breathing. Everyone else was hacking for weeks, but Dad remained untouched. We got to the point where we never knew what would happen next, but we learned to trust God's will and leave the results 100 percent to Him. God's grace gave us the faith to keep going, even when we were exhausted, frustrated, or ready to give up.

One day, Dad had us laughing after a frightening episode when his heart rate soared to the 120s. We worked frantically for several hours and eventually got the heart rate lowered to 108. As we took a few deep breaths trying to calm ourselves, we looked over at Dad. He had dragged himself out of bed and grabbed his copy of Joseph Smith's discourses.

"Ummm, what on earth are you doing, Dad??"

"I just need to pull out some quotes I was looking for the other day," he explained. "Leah needs to put them in our Google Doc."

"DAD! You are supposed to be resting?!"

With a big grin on his face, he just responded, "Man shall not live by herbs and medicines alone."

Why were we not surprised?

Dad's illness came with bouts of anxiety as his body battled to survive. Our priorities became (1) alleviate pain, (2) keep the body going, (3) let God do the rest. Oh to remember some of those terrible days! We were all learning how to become more compassionate, understanding, and patient.

Another time, his heart rate again soared for over an hour, and the anxiety was very intense. After trying *everything* we could think of, Dad cried out in exasperation: "Everyone just go. Just leave my room! I have to be alone." Hannah simply looked at Leah and Isaiah and said, "You'd better step out." They looked back and said, "Are you coming? Doesn't he need to be alone?" Hannah just smiled and said, "No, he doesn't know what he wants. It will pass, don't stress." Hannah stayed and walked Dad through the panic attack until it began to subside. When it passed, everyone came in to pray as a family and Isaiah gave Dad a blessing. When the episode was over, Dad felt crushed that he may have seemed ungrateful in telling us to leave. He was almost crying and kept apologizing. "Dad! It's fine!!" We kept trying to tell him.

Again, we didn't have a lot of options open to us so we did the best we could and tried to be content with whatever the Lord gave or took away—taking each day and each hour as it came. Managing the home, keeping up with homeschool, and Dad's care consumed the vast majority of our time. It was a miracle Dad was alive at all! During one hospital visit, a doctor said, "Mr. Stoddard, I am frankly completely amazed you are even alive." It was a season of learning complete unconditional trust in the Lord.

Word soon got around about the crazy guy with lung cancer who wouldn't "take pain killers and quit" because of his kids. Once, we went to a new hospital, though still within our network, for a heart echo test, and the technician said with a chuckle, "Wait, I know who you are! You are that dad with nine kids. We all know who you are."

Dad told the Lord he was willing to endure any amount of pain to stay for as long as possible for his kids. Hannah recorded in the cancer update log on May 31, 2021:

> Since he told God that two weeks ago, the pain has been crazy. God took him seriously. But we are learning! Watching him willing to do it for the kids, literally laying down his life. It has really challenged me. The only thing that will give you the strength to endure suffering for Christ is love. Charity is the only thing that never fails.

Charity was the crowning theme of Dad's life. He didn't believe it was initially a strength of his, and his journals are filled with prayers and pleadings with the Lord to give him this gift. Looking back at his life now, we see that it is the overarching theme—the crowning legacy he passed on to us. It was the driving motivation of his life and passion. Dad didn't give us trivial 'love' that was easy to pass out like candy. He loved when it *hurt*. As the song goes:

> *The love that asks no question, the love that stands the test*
> *That lays upon the altar, the dearest and the best*
> *The love that never falters, the love that pays the price*
> *The love that makes undaunted the final sacrifice.*[2]

Shortly after his passing, a nurse looked Hannah up on Facebook and sent her the following message. It is typical of many comments expressed to Dad by hospital staff and those who knew him during this cancer journey:

---

2   "I Vow to Thee My Country," a poem written by Sir Cecil Spring Rice. It was later adapted to the tune "Jupiter," by Gustav Holst.

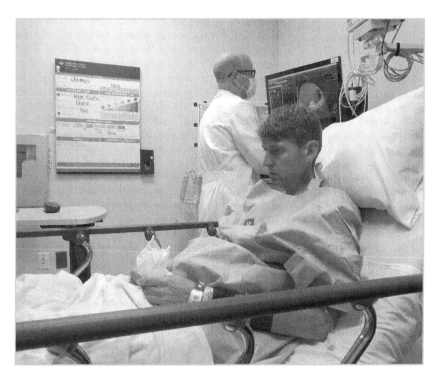

Preparing for a procedure

"Hannah- I have been thinking and wondering about your dad lately because I haven't seen him at the hospital for quite a while, and just saw his obituary that he had passed away. I'm really sorry to hear that. Ever since I first met you and your dad, the optimism, peace, and how happy you both were always amazed me. You took such great care of him and were always so pleasant. Your dad never complained, but I remember every time he came in he had to be so miserable and would always say he was doing it for one more day with his kids. I always could tell how much he loved his kids. I knew he was amazing but I read his obituary and am amazed at all the good things he had done. I just wanted to reach out because you have been on my mind and let you know that the short time I knew you both you left such a positive impression with me. I hope your family finds peace and comfort during this difficult time.

The young children of a family touched by the Joseph Smith Foundation volunteered to help weed Dad's garden & brought him a comfort box filled with snacks & other gifts.

Every time Dad went to the hospital—if the opportunity presented itself—he tried to lift and build. He would quietly listen when someone needed an ear to talk about their personal struggles or triumphs, he bore testimony of truth when appropriate, and at other times, quietly stood as an example of sincere Christianity. Walking through the hospital time and time again, we started to see life in a new way.

SEEING PAIN THROUGH NEW EYES

Hannah remembers: During the initial stay in February, I walked past a hall with a long line of floor to ceiling windows and suddenly felt compelled to stop. From the view, I could see a clinic across the street and the busy Provo street below with cars accelerating to and fro—many coming in or leaving the hospital parking lot. I saw every car, every person walking by in a completely *different* way. I turned around and looked at the families in the ICU waiting room nearby, and others coming in and out of rooms. But it was different now. It was as if I was seeing them all for the first time from a spiritual perspective. In the past, I had often recognized the spiritual pain and hurt others were feeling in my work, but now I saw the side of physical suffering. I knew what these loved ones of patients were feeling, because I was here *with* them.

I understood in a new way *why* God asks us to walk through suffering. We cannot truly and effectively serve His children without experience, without tasting the bitter. Jesus Christ knows how to help us because He has walked through all suffering—He has already passed through everything we could ever suffer. As His disciples, as those who seek to follow in His steps, we likewise are called to experience suffering so we can express true empathy, compassion, and effective service for His children who need us! That is a beautiful thing. That is true love.

The Pericardial Window Surgery, Priesthood Ordinations & More Miracles

In June, the fluid around Dad's heart had accumulated at such a rate that something needed to be done. A pericardial window surgery was proposed, where a small hole was cut in the pericardium, allowing the fluid building up to drain into the space around the right or left lung.

Some of the doctors refused to perform the procedure, because they said Dad was a lost cause. Why even try to prolong his life? However, our cardiologist advocated for us, and we were able to schedule the surgery.

The surgery was attempted on June 19, 2021. Unfortunately, they were unable to perform the procedure because, in simplified terms, his right lung had collapsed, and it was impossible to drain the fluid into the space around the left lung (his only functioning lung). The doctor told him to go home, get on the morphine, and die. While Dad was in his procedure, Isaiah and Ephraim got into

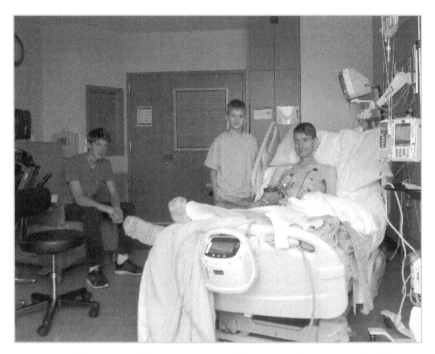

a car accident on their way to work on our homestead. Clearly protected by providence, neither of them were hurt, but it was a rough day.

We sat in the hospital feeling very defeated and not sure what to do. If Dad didn't find a way to drain the fluid from his heart, he would be dead within a few days. Dad was resting while Hannah was sitting in the hospital window with "Come Thou Fount of Every Blessing" playing from her phone. A feeling of peace came in the room—they knew God was aware, in control, and loved our family. Somehow, there was a reason this procedure had been unsuccessful, and the Lord had a plan.

Dad came home from the hospital, and we tried to be optimistic. While we were getting everything situated for the evening, Dad suddenly looked up. "This is going to sound crazy, but could you text the Bishop right now and see if there is any way I could ordain Isaiah and Ephraim on Sunday tomorrow?"

Hannah's face fell. We had been planning on Isaiah being ordained an elder and Ephraim being ordained a priest, but scheduling it the night before? Isaiah still needed the last part of his interview done. Dad had been in the middle of renewing his recommend and still needed the stake signature; how could everything be arranged? Besides, it was also Father's Day.

"I just feel like tomorrow is the only day I could possibly do it," Dad explained. He had been given all the pain medication for his surgery before the doctors realized the procedure would not work, and he knew that as long as it was in his system, he had a little time to exert the energy needed to do the ordinations.

"I was thinking around 1 p.m. would be best," Dad said. "That would give me the time to do my morning routine and also not get too late in the day." So Hannah sent a text to the bishop to see if there was any way.

When the bishop called back, we were overwhelmed by a powerful realization that God truly is sovereign over all things. Our bishop informed us that he had felt prompted several days before that Dad should ordain Isaiah and Ephraim that Sunday, and had already made all the needed arrangements—because he didn't want to approach Dad until he knew everything would work out. He had just been preparing to text when Hannah messaged!

"What time were you thinking?" we asked.

"I was hoping 1 p.m., but is that possible for you guys?" our bishop responded.

We couldn't believe our ears. Our bishop had been inspired to arrange the ordinations on the very *day*, at the very *time* Dad had needed? Talk about divine communication! We felt very humbled. The Lord was truly involved in every small detail of our lives.

That night, Dad stayed up till 10:30 p.m. talking with a young man he wanted to encourage. Dad spent the precious hours he had with some pain medication not thinking of himself, but reaching out to someone else. That is just who Dad was.

The next week, as we worked with our doctor and received advice from some other specialists, we came up with a solution for the pericardial window procedure that had failed the Saturday before. It wasn't ideal, but at least it would buy time. Usually surgeries take days and weeks to schedule, but through another coordinated set of events, a lot of Hannah's time on the phone calling doctors and nurses, and a little ingenuity, Dad was able to

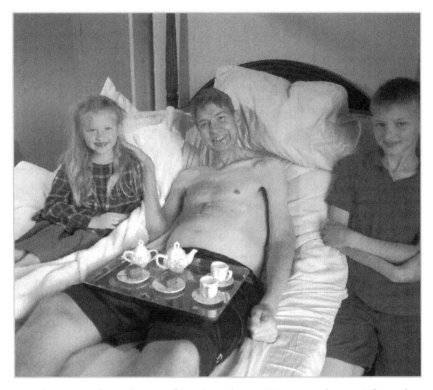

get the procedure done a few days later. We came home Thursday night and Eliza immediately seized Dad for a tea party.

We serve a God of miracles. Miracles are God's intervention to give us the grace and strength to continue progressing, growing, and becoming more like Him. Miracles are not designed to provide a life of convenience; they are not given to give us a life of ease. Our family learned to accept God's will, regardless of the outcome. And yet, even during the darkest of days—even when we felt we could not muster the courage to keep going one more hour—divine assistance was unmistakable and profound. As a family, we came closer together with a bond we had never imagined could have existed. We gained a new appreciation for the Gospel as we felt the *power* in our daily life. Every moment was important, every trial was essential, every miracle perfectly timed. We could never doubt His love and care for our family, even as we faced the realization that our Dad's time on this earth was speedily drawing to its close.

CHAPTER
Nineteen

KEEP THE FAITH

*"I have fought a good fight, I have finished my course,
I have kept the faith: Henceforth there is laid up for me
a crown of righteousness, which the Lord, the righteous
judge, shall give me at that day . . ."*

— *2 Timothy 4:7-8*

As the hot summer days passed, the understanding that Dad's mission was coming to a close began settling in on Hannah. Throughout the months of June and July, she would often lie awake at night praying for a miracle and wondering, "*How can we carry the load if Dad passes? Can we really succeed in keeping the legacy going? How hard will it be to continue alone?*"

In August, a shift occurred and she knew his time was short—Dad's work was almost done. Our focus became whatever would help him be as comfortable as possible as his life was entirely in the Lord's hands. Our family drew closer; prayer and service became more meaningful. We took shifts 24/7 since Dad could only rest in sporadic intervals and the pain required constant attendance, even while he was asleep. In the last few weeks, he was going into the clinic or hospital 3-5 times a week for a thoracentesis (each time to drain an average of 1.5 liters of pleural fluid from around his lungs). If we had an issue on the weekend, we ran to the emergency room. All the staff knew James Stoddard—the crazy guy who wouldn't quit because every day mattered for his kids.

Each day, Dad only had three priorities: survive, love his kids, and try to keep preaching the Gospel. Dad had raised his kids with these principles, but would it be enough when they were alone? Would they be able to stand entirely on their own two feet? Would they have the strength and courage to keep going?

Everyone in the family was being pushed to their limit, but instead of tearing us apart, it only made our bonds stronger—a rebirth process for each child. We gained new testimonies. Often, when we wanted to give up, past miracles would be brought to our remembrance, a friend would randomly message, or a warm feeling of love and protection confirming that the Lord was near would come to help us get through the next step. But sometimes, there were days that were long and hard, and we had to press forward believing there was light at the end of the tunnel. We had to *believe*. Looking back, light always eventually came.

In spite of excruciating pain, in the 30 days before he passed, Dad dictated two articles on scriptural teachings for sustaining leaders; he designed the male and female "I'm a Latter-day Nephite" t-shirts; he helped Hannah title and plan out presentations for the upcoming Book of Mormon Evidence Conference; he spent hours each day helping Ezra and Ephraim with their history schoolwork; he planned the upcoming Latter-day Answers Vidcast; he defended the Restoration and the Prophet Joseph Smith on social media, and he advised JSF team members on various projects. He didn't exert the energy because it was fun—it was extremely painful to keep going—but because he knew that he had consecrated his life to God and he was committed to completing his mission. Dad knew the Lord's work could only be done through His strength. On his own he was *not* enough—with or without stage 4 lung cancer.

At the end of July, Hannah asked our friends for one last fast for wisdom. Dad's health was declining, and she had big decisions to make. Dad continued enduring, and each day it became apparent why the Lord had preserved his life this long. Leah, Isaiah, Ephraim, Mary, and Ezra all underwent significant spiritual conversions during this time. On Sunday, August 29, we knew he was very close to the end. In a moment of prayer, all alone in her room, Hannah was praying when two words came distinctly to her mind: "Have faith."

The next day, Dad was still alive, but the decline continued and everyone decided the best decision would be to call an ambulance and take him to the hospital—but some of us knew this was the end. Unless he was raised like Lazarus, Dad would not be coming back home. When we arrived, staff set to work trying to stabilize his system and provide pain medication to help ease his suffering. Dad finished designing the "I'm a Latter-day Nephite" t-shirts with Leah and planned more of the upcoming expo presentations with Hannah. He cried watching videos of Afghanistan refugees attempting to flee their country. "People don't realize we and millions more scattered around the world are the literal blood of Israel," he kept telling Hannah. "I want them to know we are trying to rebuild and gather Israel in America. It's not a spiritual fairy tale. It will be a real city, with real people, real blood, and real promises. How will we gather them? With the scriptures. Tell them, Hannah. Tell them at the expo—we have to gather Israel."[1]

Faithful Footsteps

A few days before Dad passed, Hannah drove home late one night to clean up and get a fresh set of clothes and food. It was 1-2 a.m. before she was back on the road, and the gravity of the situation and approaching death of our Dad was weighing heavily on her. As she turned off Center Street in Provo, Utah—heading north down 500 W—the glowing lights of the Pedersen

---

1 Hannah Stoddard, "Refugees, Lost Israel, Zion & Awakening Freedom Fighters: Saving the Covenant & Constitution," Book of Mormon Evidence Streaming, September 2021, https://www.bookofmormonevidence.org/streaming/videos/sept-2021-expo/hannah-stoddard-refugees-lost-israel-zion-awakening-freedom-fighters-saving-the-covenant-constitution/.

Tower at the Utah Valley Hospital rose up ahead. It was like willingly walking into a nightmare, of your own free will and choice. The thought came, "You probably won't leave this hospital until it is all over, and you will never be the same again. But, *have faith*." Once again we were facing a challenge that would require all of us—but more importantly, it would require God. We couldn't do this on our own strength.

Those last days were very sacred, beautiful, and peaceful with many opportunities to share the Gospel with visitors and hospital staff. The biggest miracle was when Dad was able to see all of his kids together for the last time Saturday and Sunday night. Mom had refused to answer our texts begging her to let the kids say a final goodbye, but when one of our brothers intervened and exerted pressure, our prayers were answered. Hannah wrote in the update thread to friends and family following Dad's cancer battle:

 Yesterday was a beautiful day. Actually the last several days have certainly had their share of pain but so many tender mercies. Yesterday was the happiest he has been in weeks—all of his kids were able to gather to share a moment (which is a miracle story in and of itself because of circumstances that made us unsure whether he would be able to see four of the kids before he passed). God worked everything out! The older ones spent the afternoon with him, laughing and sharing memories (we were such crazy kids). We all knew that everything would be all right. Later in the night after he fell asleep exhausted, the nurse was watching his breathing and she said, this is the most relaxed steady breathing I have seen on him yet. God is so good. So many things have become clear and clarified in the last week for me. Every step along this journey has been a miracle, his life was preserved to accomplish everything God wanted him to do before continuing the journey in the spirit world (as Brigham Young would put it). God hurts when we hurt and He does everything He can to walk with us so we can grow and overcome every dark force in this world. This is my testimony. There is no fear in love because perfect love casts out fear.

The next hours and days will be hard, with the last struggles, but our family has had complete peace, every question answered. When I die, I want to be like him, no regrets and can honestly say, I did my best and I am not afraid to stand before God to return and report.

God has prevailed.

Over a decade before, Dad had recorded in his journal tender expressions of love for those who had given their lives in history for the testimony of the Gospel, especially those great men and women who were martyred during the Dark Ages and European Reformation. "God bless those that lived and died to bring the Gospel back into our hands," he wrote. "I hope I can die as valiantly." Now, as his final moments on earth drew near, we could each testify from experience that he did die as valiantly. We all noted the complete peace he felt—*no* regrets and not a shred of fear. Death had no sting.

As we gathered around the hospital bed Sunday night, all of us children joined our voices together in singing, "Faithful Footsteps." Dad was a born poet, had written several Christmas carols and hymns, and frequently taught us that poetic and artistic language is actually a trait of Israel—as exemplified by many ancient prophets, notably the prophet Isaiah. Back in 2005, as Dad began formulating the vision for what would eventually become the Joseph Smith Foundation, his connection to his ancestors began to deepen in new ways. Adopting the tune from *Come Thou Fount*, he poured out his feelings in poetic verse in a new hymn titled, *Faithful Footsteps*. The hymn was written to "honor all of those who have stood for truth through the last many years without station, respect or honor. Those who have quietly stood alone and been ridiculed, tortured and persecuted."

Faithful footsteps of my fathers,
Seeking ancient Truth once more.
Sacred scripture clasp'd in darkness,
Burning fire in mother-tongue.
Yoke of iron, tortured, trodden;
Dampness chills in murky gloom.
Yet a willing heart to suffer
Father's will 'till Morning's loom.

True and Faithful to His Calling
To be separate from the world.
Hunted, driven from the North Land,
Joined in cov'nant for His Word.
Born of peril, storming tempest,
Sun, nor moon, nor star canst see.
Yet Lord thou canst surely save us,
Thou hast called us to be free.

Sacred honor, lives and fortunes,
Parchment's words must never die,
Declaration, rights unalienable,
Bleeding cause, yet choice of Heav'n.
First for God, then family, country,
Millions yet, methinks I see.
But for now a voice of duty,
And the gibbet to be free.

These two prophets, sacred witness
Why from youth the called revile?
Like pure lambs going to the slaughter
They are calm as summer's morn
Sacred names had by all nations
Good or evil they must judge.
As for me, I have this witness
I praise heaven's worthy sons.

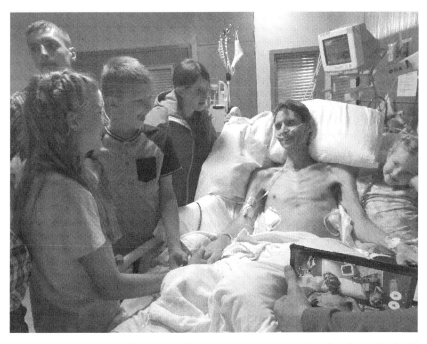

Now, as we gently sang this song together in the hospital, it became a symbolic moment. We came full circle once again as we prepared to begin a new chapter in our own lives. Could we continue walking in those faithful footsteps?

"I love you guys!"

After the kids left, Hannah and Leah stayed through the night. Dad was mostly on morphine, but we could tell he was in a lot of pain. At first, he came in and out of alertness. He would say a few words and then be unable to speak—all energy going into each breath. As the night advanced, Hannah and Leah felt scared to be alone. Unexpectedly, the hospital door room opened and two of Dad's brothers came in. The relief was inexpressible in words. They administered a final Priesthood blessing and then sat with the two girls for several hours, talking about the future, how to keep the work of the Joseph Smith Foundation going, and how to reach more people who were struggling.

Dad's final words came during the middle of the night. The morphine wore off for a moment and suddenly, he gasped up in the bed, struggling violently as he fought for each breath. As we rushed to increase his dosage, he clutched our hands and used his last ounce of strength to make sure we got this message: "Goodbye, goodbye, goodbye! I love you guys! I love you guys! I LOVE you guys!"

Then he fell back. He never spoke again, but we could tell he had said all he wanted to say. He just wanted us to know that he loved us.

Dad's brothers stayed for several hours before we convinced them to go home to their families and return in the morning. After they left, Hannah and Leah continued on together. They both felt a deep sense that this night would be one of the most difficult of their lives. One would hold Dad's hand while the other would take a short break, often to cry alone in the bathroom. At one point, Hannah was praying for help when she felt a sense of peace and understanding that everything she was going through would be used one day to help others—that this experience, this very night, was going to be used for good one day in the future. At another point, Leah took her own break and softly cried to herself, "What am I going to do without Dad? Who is going to help me now? Who am I going to talk to?" A feeling of peace came and with it the thought, "*I will always be your Dad. Whenever you need something, I will come.*"

Dad couldn't communicate with us, but we could sense there was a struggle going on. We sensed he was still alert at times and aware we were there. We played hymns throughout the night, especially his favorite, *Praise to the Man*. In the early hours of the morning, Hannah took Dad's hand and sang aloud *Faithful Footsteps*. Dad had always loved to hear us sing, but we didn't know whether he could hear us now or not. However, as she was singing, his face relaxed, and a tear came out of his right eye and fell down his face. It was a moment we would never forget.

Dad passed away peacefully the next morning at 8:47 a.m., as the sun arose on the morning of September 6 and Rosh Hashanah, the sacred Hebrew feast day also known as the Feast of Trumpets, was beginning in Palestine. Dad loved his Hebrew roots and identity as a son of Abraham, a son of Israel, and the thought that he could enjoy this celebration on the other side was comforting. As the news began to spread that he had passed, one friend sent a message:

> James' life was so full of meaning. One of the meanings for this Holy Day is "the Jewish nation recalls its responsibilities as God's chosen people." I found this is what James did for us. He helped remind us to learn our identity from God, and our responsibility as Israel. This was his life mission! His life was built on the principle of work. I can see him choosing today to die (on Labor Day) and through it saying, 'Okay, now get to work. Don't fuss over me. Be practical. No compliments. What are you going to do now that you know who you are? How are you going to tell the world?
>
> People are suffering right now because they don't know this message. So go to work! Repent of those things holding you back, those things causing you to not be who you were meant to be and do. There is no time to waste. Every minute counts.
>
> That was his message, given to all of us in LOVE! So in Hebrew tradition, the next 10 days is to evaluate your own repentance. But also ask, what are you going to do as Israel so others can awaken?

As we packed our belongings and prepared to leave the hospital for the last time there was a complete sense of peace. There was no fear. Instead, there was a calm, reassuring sense of victory; we could feel rejoicing in heaven.

On the morning of Dad's funeral, we were rushing to get ready and arrive in time for the viewing when we heard a group of neighborhood kids yelling outside in the street to their friends, "Look at the rainbow!" Curious, we peeked outside the window, and before our eyes was the most beautiful, brilliant double rainbow right over us—and we cried. During one of

Dad's hospital procedures, a large brilliant rainbow had come over our farm while we were praying, and we had felt it was a tender reminder to not lose hope. The funeral rainbow felt like a second witness—God's promises were sure, everything was going according to His plan, and He was in control. The torch had been passed to the next generation—now it was our responsibility to "keep the faith."

Keep the Faith

Dad had three simple requests for the funeral arrangements: (1) an inexpensive white casket; (2) all funeral talks should bear testimony of Jesus Christ and the Gospel through personal experience—no bragging and no sermonizing; and finally, (3) he wanted his headstone to bear two scriptures:

 I have no greater joy than to hear that my children walk in truth. (3 John 1:4)

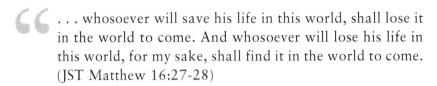 . . . whosoever will save his life in this world, shall lose it in the world to come. And whosoever will lose his life in this world, for my sake, shall find it in the world to come. (JST Matthew 16:27-28)

Dad had found the secret to true joy—and he taught us well. He lived what he preached. His legacy and service were no accident—he did this work because he *chose* this path intentionally and without looking back.

Dad understood that if fathers and mothers build a Christ-centered home, they will make an invaluable impact on the world for good. Pay the price to produce a family team—building a legacy that will last many generations. As we drove away from the hospital, we felt a sting of sadness, but we didn't feel *fear*. We are confident to move forward, because our trust was not in Dad. He was not the Rock, he was not our foundation. Dad taught us to place our foundation in Jesus Christ. None of our work was done for Dad—it was done for the Lord—and whether Dad is here in the flesh, or working on the other side of the veil, truth will prevail.

Whenever we left the home or parted while growing up, Dad's famous farewell line was the phrase: "Keep the faith!" As we look back over our lives, we have one last message we want to give in return.

You don't need to worry, Dad! Your kids *will* carry on this legacy—we will NOT let it die! The message you began of hope and healing through the Gospel of Jesus Christ will not be neglected or lost. We will remember what you taught us, and we are so grateful for your example. We are *proud* to be your kids—to be the children of James Stoddard—and we will carry the standard of truth to the world.

We will keep the faith.

James Franklin Stoddard III (1970-2021)

L. HANNAH STODDARD, AUTHOR

L. Hannah Stoddard is the lead author of *Faith Crisis, Volume 1: We Were NOT Betrayed!*, *Faith Crisis, Volume 2: Behind Closed Doors, Joseph Smith's Plural Wives, Volume 1: Helen Mar Kimball*, and *Seer Stone v. Urim & Thummim: Book of Mormon Translation on Trial*. She is the executive director of the Joseph Smith Foundation and the producer or director of seven documentary feature films.

- Nephites in Europe (Episodes 1 & 2, Quest for the Nephite Remnant) (2019)
- Hidden Bloodlines: The Grail & the Lost Tribes in the Lands of the North (2017)
- Unlocking the Mystery of the Two Prophets: Revelation 11 (2017)
- The Prophet Joseph: More than we know (2015)
- Statesmen & Symbols: Prelude to the Restoration (2014)
- For Our Day: Divinely Sanctioned Governments (2013)
- For Our Day: Covenant on the Land (2013)

In addition to directing Joseph Smith Foundation projects for over a decade, she is often invited to speak on various radio and video programs. Beginning at age 16, Hannah helped direct her first documentary film. She has worked as a history and literature teacher, graphic design artist, software developer, videographer, project manager, agriculturist, and research assistant. Her work focuses on Church history and doctrine, answers to Latter-day Saint faith crisis questions, educational philosophy, culture, and defending the Prophet Joseph Smith. Hannah's research supports the writings and teachings of ancient and latter-day prophets.

LEAH M. STODDARD, AUTHOR

Leah M. Stoddard is a citation editor, lead animator, graphic designer, sound designer for the Joseph Smith Foundation. She was interviewed in the documentary, *Hidden Bloodlines: The Grail & the Lost Tribes in the Lands of the North*. She also contributes through research, editing, web development, and more. In her free time, Leah enjoys animal husbandry, cooking, art, music, studying Gospel topics, and working at their family-owned perennial garden retreat. Leah is excited about working with her siblings and establishing a multigenerational vision.

ISAIAH M. STODDARD, AUTHOR

Isaiah McConkie Stoddard is an information technology specialist for the Joseph Smith Foundation. Additionally, he is skilled in web development, video production, research, graphics animation, DVD menu design, and sound effect editing. He particularly enjoys studying issues associated with the gospel, faith crisis answers, and Church history. Isaiah began taking college courses at age 16 where he specifically studied computer programming and cyber defense—winning several awards. In his free time, he enjoys working on their family homestead, Highland Cathedral Estate, where they experiment with farming techniques and perennial food production.

Nephites in Europe Documentary

(Episodes 1 & 2) Quest for the Nephite Remnant

Winner, 2nd Place—LDS Film Festival Feature Documentary—2020

For over a century and a half, we assumed the Nephites struggled to extinction. What if remnants escaped to Europe, Japan, New Zealand, Burma, etc.–to become nations, kindreds, tongues, and people? An ancient Icelandic text records a royal family in Northern Europe descending from a prince by the name of Nefi or Nephi. Another Northern European tribe was known by a name that likely means the "people of Nephi." Did Nephites travel to Europe?

Episode 1: Nephites in Europe

An ancient Icelandic text records a royal family in Northern Europe descending from a prince by the name of Nefi or Nephi. Another Northern European tribe was known by a name that likely means the "people of Nephi." Did Nephites travel to Europe?

Episode 2: Nephite Survivors in Prophecy

Did righteous Nephite families escape and spread throughout the world? Was Joseph Smith a descendant of Joseph, son of Lehi? Why did the Lord tell Joseph Smith that the Book of Mormon would be given to Latter-day Nephites, Jacobites, Josephites, and Zoramites as well as Lamanites, Lemuelites, and Ishmaelites?

Guest Appearances: John D. Nelson, Scott N. Bradley, Timothy Ballard

RUNTIME: 1 HR 2 MIN

Order now at www.JosephSmithFoundation.org
or watch on Amazon Prime

JOSEPH SMITH FOUNDATION DOCUMENTARIES
www.JosephSmithFoundation.org

Statesmen & Symbols: Prelude to the Restoration

What do LDS temples have in common with the Great Pyramid of Giza, Stonehenge, and the Hopewell mounds in North America? Why are some of the sacred symbols used by the Founding Fathers also found on tapestries in China that date to the time of the flood? What are the details of American Founding Father Benjamin Rush's vision concerning Thomas Jefferson and John Adams?

Unlocking the Mystery of the Two Prophets: Revelation 11

Who are the two prophets in Revelation 11, the two messengers who lie dead in the great city? An assassination by enemies, a forbidden burial by persecutors, and bodies lying in the street for three and a half days are only a few of the clues found in scripture revealing their identity. The two prophets have generally been shrouded in mystery . . . until now.

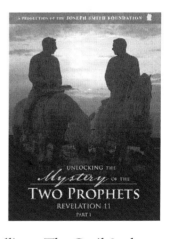

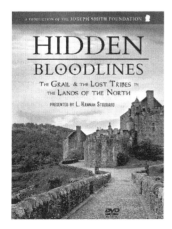

Hidden Bloodlines: The Grail & the Lost Tribes in the Lands of the North

Winner, 3rd Place
LDS Film Festival Feature Documentary—2018

The legendary search for the Holy Grail has resonated with millions for centuries! What is the Holy Grail, and why is this legendary symbol important to the lives of Joseph Smith and the Son of God? Was Jesus Christ married and did He have children? Discover your own heritage, your own royal birthright, in a way you may never have imagined!

JOSEPH SMITH FOUNDATION DOCUMENTARIES

www.JosephSmithFoundation.org

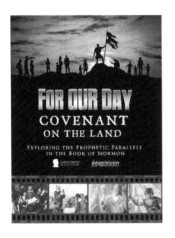

For Our Day: Covenant on the Land

This film discusses the covenant on the Promised Land for both ancient and modern inhabitants, presenting inspiring history from the American colonization, paralleling the Puritans, Pilgrims and other righteous forebears with Lehi, Nephi and the first part of the Book of Mormon. Is latter-day history laid out and foreshadowed in the Book of Mormon?

For Our Day: Divinely Sanctioned Governments

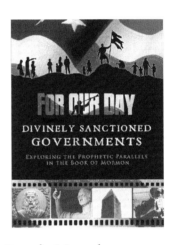

This film compares the Nephite and Latter-day governments of liberty, covering principles of liberty including: Unalienable Rights, Oath of Office, Federalism, the U.S. and Hebrew connection, as well as the Laws of Mosiah. This feature documentary adds an understanding of governmental principles as they are taught in the most correct book, the Book of Mormon.

The Prophet Joseph: More than we know

Ground-breaking research on latter-day prophecy! Is the Prophet Joseph the Angel in Revelation 14, the designator of Zion inheritances, the Messenger in Malachi, the Servant in Isaiah, the passport to Celestial glory, the Voice crying in the wilderness? Discover the Prophet Joseph Smith in a way you have never imagined!